ARTISTIK PARIS

Written by
Natasha Edwards

Illustrated by
Alain Bouldouyre

AUTHENTIK BOOKS

Les Editions du Mont Tonnerre
4 bis Villa du Mont-Tonnerre
Paris XVe arrondissement

AUTHENTIK®

Published by The Globe Pequot Press
246 Goose Lane, P.O. Box 480
Guilford, Connecticut 06437
www.globepequot.com

© 2008 Authentik Books
www.authentikbooks.com

Produced in France by Les Editions du Mont-Tonnerre
Text and illustrations copyright © Wilfried LeCarpentier

Authentik® Trademark, Wilfried LeCarpentier
4 bis Villa du Mont-Tonnerre, Paris XVe arrondissement
www.monttonnerre.com

ISBN 978-0-7627-4637-8
First Edition

Printed and bound in China

LES EDITIONS DU MONT-TONNERRE
Founder and Publisher: Wilfried LeCarpentier
Editor-at-Large: William Landmark
Managing Editor: Caroline Favreau

AUTHENTIK ARTISTIK PARIS
Restaurants, Wine and Food Consultant: Gérard Poirot
Project Editor: Nicola Mitchell
Copy Editors: Jessica Fortescue and Helen Stuart
Proofreader: Carly Jane Lock
Researcher: Jessica Phelan
Editorial Assistant: Jennifer Parker

Creative Director: Lorenzo Locarno
Artistic Director: Nicolas Mamet
Graphic Designer: Amélie Dommange
Layout Artist: Marie-Thérèse Gomez
Cover Design and Packaging: Nicolas Mamet
Cartographer: Map Resources
Map Illustrator: Kouakou
Pre-Press and Production: Studio Graph'M, Montrouge

GLOBE PEQUOT PRESS
President and Publisher: Scott Watrous
Editorial Director: Karen Cure

ACKNOWLEDGEMENTS

Special thanks to Marie-Christine Levet, Scott Watrous, Karen Cure, Gunnar Stenmar, Gérard Paulin, Pierre Jovanovic, Jacques Derey, Bruno de sa Moreira, Ian Irvine, Laura Tennant, Francesco Betti and Charles Walker

Uncover the Exceptional

The Authentik book collection was born out of a desire to explore beauty and craftsmanship in every domain and in whatever price bracket. The books describe the aesthetic essence of a city, homing in on modern-day artisans who strive for perfection and whose approach to their work is as much spiritual as commercial. Written by specialist authors, the guides delve deep into the heart of a capital and, as a result, are excellent companions for both locals and nomadic lovers of fine living. Their neat size, made to fit into a suit or back pocket, make them easy and discreet to consult, and their elegant design and insider selection of addresses will ensure that you get to the heart of the local scene and blend in perfectly with it. There is even a notebook at the back for some cerebral scribbling of your own. In all, Authentik Books are the perfect accessory for uncovering the exceptional, whether in the arts, fashion, design or gastronomy.

Wilfried LeCarpentier
Founder and Publisher

Contents

How to Use This Guide

Ever felt like jumping in a taxi at Roissy airport and saying, "Take me to the centre of things!?" Well, this book does the work of a very knowledgeable taxi driver.

Artistik Paris consists of ten chapters of insider information on the capital's thriving arts scene. Besides highlighting the unmissable mainstream destinations, the guide ventures into little known insider territories: the open studios, the small but influential galleries and edgy performance spaces. There's even information on where to study should you decide to stay in the city and feed the artist in you.

The directory at the end of each chapter gives the addresses of the places mentioned, plus the details of other essential stops too numerous to include in the chapter. The maps at the back of the guide cover the principal streets of central Paris. Use the map references added to the addresses to find the general location of our listings.

Using the **2D BAR CODE** below you can load all the addresses onto a mobile phone with Internet access. This unique aspect of the book enables you to travel extra light.

scan here

How to access content on your mobile phone

If your mobile phone has Internet access and a built-in camera go to
www.scanlife.com
Download the free software that allows your mobile phone to identify the bar code. Downloading takes less than one minute. Then go to your personal file icon, which will appear on your phone's menu screen, and select the icon **Scanlife**. Next, point your camera at the 2D bar code. A sound confirms that the bar code has been recognized. You can then access the directories on your phone.

AN APPETITE
FOR CULTURE

Palais Garnier
place de l'Opéra, 9th

Previous page: Palais de Tokyo
13 avenue du Président Wilson, 16th

Paris is a city synonymous with art and culture. Moreover, despite the enormous weight of France's architectural and artistic heritage, there is also a true appetite for the contemporary. Behind the golden stone facades of its beautiful *hôtel particuliers*, and apartment blocks designed by French civic planner Baron Georges-Eugène Haussmann, lie countless studios, alleyways and converted industrial buildings that serve as a creative cauldron of artists, designers and writers, filmmakers and dancers.

The intellectual remains a prized species in France and at any one time the city offers an incredible choice of concerts and performances to listen to and an enviable array of museums and art collections to visit. Each autumn sees an enormous outpouring of new books for the literary *rentrée* (the return from holidays in September). Audiences continue to flock to experimental theatre productions. The **Opéra National de Paris**, **Théâtre du Châtelet** and **Opéra Comique** all show a commitment to creating new opera, and experimental music institute **IRCAM**, the Insitut de Recherche et Coordination Acoustique/Musique, provides a unique bridge between avant-garde classical and electronic music. Art venues like the **Palais de Tokyo** and **Centre Pompidou** are equally engaged in contemporary creation, with crossovers between video and dance, art and music.

Institutions like the **Centre Pompidou** and the **FRAC**s, or regional foundations for contemporary art, remain dominant in the art market, but there is also a nucleus of private collectors that is slowly becoming more visible, thanks to initiatives like the **Maison Rouge** and the Prix Marcel Duchamp. Commercial galleries and public institutions work side by side. If it's the museums that put on the prestigious exhibitions, it is the galleries that work over the long term with an artist, putting confidence in their work and seeing them through a project. If you want to get a feel of this art world buzz, head to the northern Marais or rue Louise-Weiss on a vernissage night, when artists, collectors, curators, critics and enthusiasts congregate for the gallery openings.

La Nuit Blanche each October shows it is possible to widen the audience for contemporary art, with daring installations and video projections in open air sites around Paris. An opinion poll published in *Beaux-Arts* magazine showed that a majority of French people saw themselves as at least "curious" about contemporary art, and under-35s placed it before historic art.

Paris is also at the heart of Europe's biggest film industry. Barely a day goes by when you won't come across a film being shot somewhere in the city, but it also remains a capital for cinephiles where you can find an incredible variety of international films screened in their own language.

Creative boundaries

So where do you find Paris's creative hub today? There's been a geographical shift. Rising rents and property prices and changes in art production itself mean that you can no longer – if you ever could – make the old Left Bank-intellectuals-and-artists and Right Bank-business-and-commerce divide. As Saint-Germain-des-Prés and the Latin Quarter have become more prosperous and bourgeois, some of their creative dynamism seems to have shifted northeastwards to the 11th or the 20th *arrondissements*, home to artists and a vibrant bar culture. At the same time, some myths are self-perpetuating: Saint-Germain retains a gravitational pull, and its cafés and brasseries continue to be the places for those who have made it to see and be seen. Attempts to take culture beyond the *beaux-quartiers* have not necessarily widened the avant-garde audience: it is still largely Paris's chattering classes who flock to the state supported suburban theatres at Bobigny and Créteil during the **Festival d'Automne** or to productions by Peter Brook at the **Bouffes du Nord**.

Théâtre des Bouffes du Nord
37 bis boulevard de la Chapelle, 10th

Artists studios

It's only natural that the artistic boundaries of the city have shifted. Paris is a much bigger conurbation than it was a century ago. Although the original artists studios scattered throughout Montmartre and the Montparnasse fringes tend to have become chic loft-style apartments, northeast Paris is home to many artists studios. Other artists have migrated to the inner suburbs – Montreuil to the east, Saint-Denis and Aubervilliers to the north, Vanves, Montrouge and Ivry-sur-Seine to the south – places that are rapidly connected to the centre by the Métro, but where there are lower rents and more of the sort of old industrial spaces suitable for converting into studios.

If the artistic scene is less visible than it was in the early 20th century, that is also because the position of contemporary creation is all-encompassing, and art production itself constantly in question. Today, artists are much less likely to be found standing behind an easel, and one of the signs of Paris's creative vitality is the proliferation of multidisciplinary crossovers, collaborations between dancers and video artists, artists and musicians. Go out and discover.

CONTEMPORARY ART GALLERIES

Ateliers d'Artistes de Belleville
32 rue de la Mare, 20th

Prévious page: Pièce Unique
4 rue Jacques Callot, 6th

02

The Parisian art scene remains vibrantly international. Galleries reflect an art culture where ideas, trends and the artists themselves move effortlessly among countries and media. While installation and video remain prominent, painting continues to thrive, despite frequent declarations of its death, and there is growing interest in drawing as seen in the first Salon du Dessin Contemporain in 2007. Check out what's on in the Galeries Mode d'Emploi and Association des Galeries leaflets found in galleries and on the websites www.associationdesgaleries.org and www.paris-art.com.

The Marais art hub

Paris's contemporary galleries are concentrated around Beaubourg and the northern Marais. Essential stops include **Galerie Chantal Crousel**, which features the spectacular installations of Paris-based Swiss artist Thomas Hirschhorn and video works by Melik Ohanian and Anri Sala. Another powerhouse is **Galerie Yvon Lambert**, where major names like Anselm Kiefer, Andres Serrano and Jenny Holzer can be found alongside the younger generation. Dynamic **Galerie Emmanuel Perrotin** is the place to pick up on trends including Takashi Murakami and the Japanese manga tribe, Austrian collective Gellatin, German painter Peter Zimmermann and French art ranging from Sophie Calle's photo-text pieces to Lionel Estève's string constructions. Another influential gallery is **Chez Valentin**, whose shows have an offbeat conceptual edge.

Galerie Daniel Templon concentrates on painters, including France's Jean-Michel Alberola and Gérard Garouste, as well as American figurative artists and the new generation of German painters. **Galerie Marian Goodman**'s elegant space features American artists such as Jeff Wall, and European video makers Chantal Ackermann and Eija-Liisa Ahtila. Big, bankable international names also tend to be found at the Paris outpost of **Karsten Grève**, while **Thaddaeus Ropac** often features neo-Pop artists such as Alex Katz and Tom Sachs. **Galerie Almine Rech** highlights artists such as Ugo Rondinone, James Turrell and Ange Leccia in an apartment setting.

More recent arrivals include **Galerie Jean Brolly**, showing mainly paintings and works on paper, and **Galerie Laurent Godin**, with shows varying from the hip newspaper installations of Wang Du and series fanatic Claude Closky to mixed media works by young artists Vincent Olinet and Delphine Coindet.

Galerie Anne de Villepoix demonstrates the eclecticism of contemporary art with monochrome paintings by Dijon-based Chinese artist Ming, simulacra and videos by Franck Scurti and South African photographer Zwetethu Mthetwa. **Galerie Cent8** is equally eclectic. Other places to see emerging artists include **Schleicher + Lange**, which showcases talents from Eastern Europe and Britain, **Galerie Alain Gutharc**, **Galerie Maisonneuve**, and active, young **Galerie Magda Danysz.**

The Champs-Elysées: modern masters

As befits the area, galleries near the Champs-Elysées tend to show established international artists and woo private and corporate buyers: Jannis Kounellis and Sean Scully at **Galerie Lelong**; classic moderns and *nouvelle figuration* at **Louis Carré**; and photo duo Pierre et Gilles and Eva and Adele, the self-styled Hermaphrodite Twins in Art, at **Jérôme de Noirmont.**

Saint-Germain-des-Prés: contemporary mix

The traditional gallery heartland of Saint-Germain has become rather staid, with a clutch of small galleries geared to traditional modern art, Art Deco furniture and tribal art. Yet there are some excellent exceptions: at **Galerie Lara Vincy**, you'll find the odd art happening-type event, while some more experimental galleries have begun to make their mark.

Air de Paris
32 rue Louise Weiss, 13th

Galerie Georges-Philippe & Nathalie Vallois regularly presents French artists Alain Bublex, Boris Achour and Gilles Barbier. **Galerie Kamel Mennour** started off primarily showing photos by Peter Beard and Nobuyoshi Araki but is now better known for high-profile, sometimes political, young French artists Kader Attia and Adel Abdessemed. **Galerie Loevenbruck** supports an eclectic group, including the neo-Surrealist paintings and objects of Philippe Mayaux, winner of the 2006 Prix Marcel Duchamp. **Pièce Unique** is an unusual one-off: each show consists of a specially commissioned work, which you view through the glass shopfront.

02

Louise: a new district

Created in 1997, Louise is an association of contemporary galleries in the new-build 13th *arrondissement*, with an emphasis on emerging artists and a policy of shared vernissage opening nights. Worth looking out for are the trendy conceptual and fashion-world artists at **Air de Paris**, **In Situ**, young artists at **gb agency**, design gallery **Galerie Kreo** and **Jousse Entreprise** with its mix of young artists and classic modern furniture.

Photography galleries

Many galleries include photography, but a few are dedicated to the art. At **Galerie Anne Barrault**, young European photographers include Philippe Bazin,

La Chambre Claire
14 rue Saint Sulpice, 6th

Hop on the art bus

Once a month, some 35 art enthusiasts pile into the **Navette de l'Art Contemporain** (Art Bus), a convivial, day-long guided tour of happening galleries, art centres, apartment galleries and a few private collections. Arranged by Art Process, it's a good way to discover insider addresses and to meet the artists. Since being set up in 1998 by critic Eric Mézan, the tours have expanded to Brussels and London, along with "Dining with..." art dinners at the Point Ephémère, made-to-measure tours in the chauffeured Art Limousine, and the Art Bus's new design sibling, the Buzz Bus. **Navette de l'Art Contemporain**, Art Process, 52 rue Sedaine, 11th; M° Bastille, tel: 01 47 00 90 85; www.art-process.com.

Katharina Bosse and Gabriele Basilico, at **Galerie Polaris**, you should look for Stéphane Couturier's extraordinary building site series. **Françoise Paviot** features both vintage and contemporary photography; while **Agathe Gaillard** tends towards classic black-and-white and documentary images. Photo bookshop **La Chambre Claire** puts on exhibitions in the basement.

02

Design and interiors

Design is on a roll in Paris, where designers such as Erwan and Ronan Bouroullec, Martin Szekely, Christophe Pillet and RADI Designers vary commercial work with limited editions and experimental items for galleries such as **FR66**, Galerie Kreo (*see page 25*) and **Tools Galerie**. **Gilles Peyroulet & Cie** features artists as well as avant-garde design by Aalto and Eileen Gray and crossover projects by contemporary designers. The **Lieu Commun** shop is a shared initiative by designer Matali Crasset, fashion stylist Ron Orb and electronic music label F.Com, where you'll find Crasset's furniture and glasses alongside clothes and CDs.

Galerie Patrick Seguin and Jousse Entreprise (*see page 25)* are the places to find 20th-century furniture classics by Prouvé, Le Corbusier, Periand and Royère, ceramics by Georges Jouve and the multi-branch metal lamps of Serge Mouille. **Galerie Doria** has a near monopoly on furniture by Pierre Chareau, the architect of Modernist icon the Maison de Verre. At **Galerie Downtown**, François Affanour mixes Perriand, Carlo Mollino and 1950s items with limited editions by Ron Arad. In Montmartre **Christine Diegoni** features lighting by Gino Sarfatti alongside 1950s and 1960s American design by George Nelson and Charles and Ray Eames.

Tribal art and emerging nations

France leads the primitive art market, spurred by some important auctions and the opening of the Musée du Quai Branly, with specialist galleries concentrated in Saint-Germain-des-Prés. **Galerie Alain Lecomte** focuses on African work. **Galerie Flak** has pieces from North America, Africa and Australasia, along with Brazilian furniture from the 1950s to 1970s, plus photography and rare books. **Galerie Monbrison** covers Africa, Australasia and North America. More contemporary African artists are less well represented, although some, such as Barthélémy Toguo, have become part of the international art circuit and can be found at galleries such as Anne de Villepoix *(see page 23)*. The **Musée des Arts Derniers** in the Marais is more specifically dedicated to promoting contemporary art from Africa, while Stéphane Jacob at **Arts d'Australie** champions aboriginal art, ranging from traditional bark paintings to more international-style acrylics.

Prints, editions and art books

Artists editions, as showcased by the adventurous artist-run **Galerie de Multiples**, can take pretty much any form, from lithographs to ceramics, resin soup ladles to music. **Christophe Daviet-Thery** maintains the more classic tradition of limited edition artists books. **Studio Franck Bordas** has moved from litho-graphy to collaborations with artists using new digital technology. **Florence Loewy** gathers art books, artists editions and posters as well as exploring crossovers with music. Pioneering lifestyle store **Colette** features ultra-cool artists' limited editions, such as a running shoe by Claude Closky, rare art magazines, and exhibitions. Check out also the quirky Japanese kitsch, artists' editions and tee-shirts displayed in fridges at **BlackBlock**, inside the Palais de Tokyo.

02

Studio visits

Open-studio weekends, known as Portes Ouvertes, generally held in May or early autumn, can be a good way to meet artists in their working environment. The longest established is **Le Génie de la Bastille**; the largest, with more than 200 participating artists across the 11th, 19th and 20th *arrondissements*, is the **Ateliers des Artistes à Belleville**, while **Les Frigos**, a bunch of studios in graffiti-strewn former refrigerated warehouses, has become a vital element of the Rive Gauche development zone.

Avenue Matignon, 8th

The Marais art hub

Chez Valentin
9 r St Gilles, 3rd
Ⓜ Chemin Vert
📞 01 48 87 42 55
galeriechezvalentin.com
🧭 12/U11

Galerie Alain Gutharc
7 r St Claude, 3rd
Ⓜ St Sébastien Froissart
📞 01 47 00 32 10
alaingutharc.com
🧭 12/U10

Galerie Almine Rech
19 r de Saintonge, 3rd
Ⓜ St Sébastien Froissart
📞 01 45 83 71 90
galeriealminerech.com
🧭 7-8/T9

**Galerie Anne
de Villepoix**
43 r de Montmorency, 3rd
Ⓜ Rambuteau
Ⓒ 01 42 78 32 24
annedevillepoix.com
✣ 7/R9

Galerie Cent 8
108 r Vieille-du-Temple, 3rd
Ⓜ St Sébastien Froissart
Ⓒ 01 42 74 53 57
cent8.com
✣ 11-12/T10

Galerie Chantal Crousel
10 r Charlot, 3rd
Ⓜ Filles du Calvaire
Ⓒ 01 42 77 38 87
crousel.com
✣ 7-8/T9

Galerie Daniel Templon
30 r Beaubourg, 3rd
Ⓜ Rambuteau
Ⓒ 01 42 72 14 10
danieltemplon.com
✣ 7/R9

**Galerie Emmanuel
Perrotin**
76 r de Turenne, 3rd
Ⓜ St Sébastien Froissart
Ⓒ 01 42 16 79 79
galerieperrotin.com
✣ 12/U10

Galerie Jean Brolly
16 r de Montmorency, 3rd
Ⓜ Rambuteau
Ⓒ 01 42 78 88 02
jeanbrolly.com
✣ 7/R9

Galerie Laurent Godin
5 r du Grenier St Lazare, 3rd
Ⓜ Rambuteau
Ⓒ 01 42 71 10 66
laurentgodin.com
✣ 7/R9

Galerie Magda Danysz
78 r Amelot, 11th
Ⓜ Filles du Calvaire
Ⓒ 01 45 83 38 51
magda-gallery.com
✣ 12/U10

Galerie Maisonneuve
22 r de Poitou, 3rd
Ⓜ St Sébastien Froissart
Ⓒ 01 43 66 23 99.
galerie-maisonneuve.com
✣ 11-12/T10

Galerie Marian Goodman
79 r du Temple, 3rd
Ⓜ Rambuteau
Ⓒ 01 48 04 70 52
mariangoodman.com
✣ 11-12/R10

Galerie Michel Rein
42 r de Turenne, 3rd
Ⓜ Chemin Vert
Ⓒ 01 42 72 68 132
michelrein.com
✣ 12/U11

Galerie Yvon Lambert
108 r Vieille-du-Temple, 3rd
Ⓜ St Sébastien Froissart
Ⓒ 01 42 71 09 33
yvon-lambert.com
✣ 11-12/T10

Karsten Grève
5 r Debelleyme, 3rd
Ⓜ St Sébastien Froissart
Ⓒ 01 42 77 19 37
artnet.com/kgreve-paris.
html
✣ 11-12/T10

Schleicher + Lange
12 r de Picardie, 3rd
Ⓜ Filles du Calvaire
Ⓒ 01 42 77 02 77
schleicherlange.com
✣ 7-8/T9

Thaddaeus Ropac
7 r Debelleyme, 3rd
Ⓜ St Sébastien Froissart
Ⓒ 01 42 72 99 00
ropac.net
✣ 11-12/T10

02

Studio visits

**Ateliers des Artistes
de Belleville**
32 r de la Mare, 20th
Ⓜ Pyrénées
Ⓒ 01 46 36 44 09
ateliers-artistes-belleville.org
⊕ 8/Z6

Les Frigos
19 r des Frigos, 13th
Ⓜ Bibliothèque
les-frigos.com
⊕ Off map

Le Génie de la Bastille
11th and 12th
Ⓜ Bastille
legeniedelabastille.net
⊕ 12/V13

Prints, editions and art books

BlackBlock
Palais de Tokyo, 13 av du
Président Wilson, 16th
Ⓜ Iéna
Ⓒ 01 47 23 37 04
blackblock.org
⊕ 5/D9

Colette
213 r St-Honoré, 1st
Ⓜ Tuileries
Ⓒ 01 55 35 33 90
colette.fr
⊕ 6/L8

Galerie de Multiples
17 r St Gilles, 3rd
Ⓜ Chemin Vert
Ⓒ 01 48 87 21 77
galeriedemultiples.com
⊕ 12/U11

Christophe Daviet-Thery
10 r Duchefdelaville, 13th
Ⓜ Chevaleret
Ⓒ 01 53 79 05 95
daviet-thery.com
⊕ Off map

Florence Loewy
9 r de Thorigny, 3rd
Ⓜ St Sébastien Froissart
Ⓒ 01 44 78 98 45
florenceloewy.com
⊕ 11-12/T10

Studio Franck Bordas
(by appointment)
Ⓒ 01 47 00 31 61
franckbordas.online.fr

The Champs-Elysées: modern masters

Galerie Lelong
13 r de Téhéran, 8th
Ⓜ Miromesnil
Ⓒ 01 45 63 13 19
galerie-lelong.com
⊕ 2/H4

Jérôme de Noirmont
36-38 av Matignon, 8th
Ⓜ Miromesnil
Ⓒ 01 42 89 89 00
denoirmont.com
⊕ 6/H7

Louis Carré
10 av de Messine, 8th
Ⓜ Miromesnil
Ⓒ 01 45 62 57 07
louiscarre.fr
⊕ 2/H4

Louise: a new district

Air de Paris
32 r Louise Weiss, 13th
Ⓜ Chevaleret
Ⓒ 01 44 23 02 77
airdeparis.com
⊕ Off map

Galerie Kreo
22 r Duchefdelaville, 13th
Ⓜ Chevaleret
Ⓒ 01 53 60 18 42
galeriekreo.com
⊕ Off map

In Situ
10 r Duchefdelaville, 13th
Ⓜ Chevaleret
Ⓒ 01 53 79 06 12
insituparis.fr
⊕ Off map

Galerie Art Concept
16 r Duchefdelaville, 13th
Ⓜ Chevaleret
Ⓒ 01 53 60 90 30
galerieartconcept.com
⊕ Off map

gb agency
20 r Louise Weiss, 13th
Ⓜ Chevaleret
Ⓒ 01 53 79 07 13
gbagency.fr
⊕ Off map

Jousse Entreprise
24 r Louise Weiss, 13th
Ⓜ Chevaleret
Ⓒ 01 53 82 10 18
jousse-entreprise.com
⊕ Off map

02

Photography galleries

Agathe Gaillard
3 r du Pont Louis-
Philippe, 4th
Ⓜ Pont Marie
Ⓒ 01 42 77 38 24
agathegaillard.com
⊕ 11/R12

Françoise Paviot
57 r Ste Anne, 2nd
Ⓜ Quatre Septembre
Ⓒ 01 42 60 10 01
paviotfoto.com
⊕ 12/U10

**Galerie Michèle
Chomette**
24 r Beaubourg, 3rd
Ⓜ Rambuteau
Ⓒ 01 42 78 05 62
⊕ 7/R9

La Chambre Claire
14 r St Sulpice, 6th
Ⓜ Odéon
Ⓒ 01 46 34 04 31
chambreclaire.com
⊕ 11/N13

Galerie Anne Barrault
22 r St Claude, 3rd
Ⓜ St Sébastien Froissart
Ⓒ 01 44 78 91 67
galerieannebarault.com
⊕ 12/U10

Galerie Polaris
15 r des Arquebusiers, 3rd
Ⓜ St Sébastien Froissart
Ⓒ 01 42 72 21 27
galeriepolaris.com
⊕ 12/U10

Galerie Meyer Oceanic Art
17 rue des Beaux Arts, 6th

Design and interiors

Christine Diegoni
47 r d'Orsel, 18th
Ⓜ Abbesses
Ⓒ 01 42 64 69 48
christinediegoni.fr
⊕ 3/O2

FR66
25 r de Renard, 4th
Ⓜ Hôtel de Ville
Ⓒ 01 44 54 35 36
fr66.com
⊕ 11/R11

Galerie Doria
16 r de Seine, 6th
Ⓜ Mabillon
Ⓒ 01 43 25 43 25
⊕ 11/N12

Galerie Downtown
33 r de Seine, 6th
Ⓜ Mabillon
Ⓒ 01 46 33 82 41
galeriedowntown.com
⊕ 11/N12

Galerie Patrick Seguin
5 r des Taillandiers, 11th
Ⓜ Ledru Rollin
Ⓒ 01 47 00 32 35
patrickseguin.com
⊕ 12/W12

Gilles Peyroulet & Cie
80 r Quincampoix, 3rd
Ⓜ Rambuteau
Ⓒ 01 42 78 85 11
⊕ 7/Q9

Lieu Commun
5 r des Filles du Calvaire, 3rd
Ⓜ Filles du Calvaire
Ⓒ 01 44 54 08 30
lieucommun.fr
⊕ 8/U9

Tools Galerie
119 r Vieille du Temple, 3rd
Ⓜ Filles du Calvaire
Ⓒ 01 42 77 35 80
toolsgalerie.com
⊕ 11-12/T10

VIA
29 av Daumesnil, 12th
Ⓜ Gare de Lyon
Ⓒ 01 46 28 11 11
via.fr
⊕ 16/W15

Tribal art and emerging nations

Arts d'Australie
(by appointment)
ⓒ 01 46 22 23 20
artsdaustralie.com

Galerie Flak
8 r des Beaux Arts, 6th
Ⓜ St-Germain-des-Prés
ⓒ 01 46 33 77 77
galerieflak.com
⊕ 11/N12

Galerie Monbrison
2 r des Beaux Arts, 6th
Ⓜ Mabillon
ⓒ 01 46 34 05 20
monbrison.com
⊕ 11/N12

02

Galerie Alain Lecomte
21 r Guénégaud, 6th
Ⓜ Odéon
a 01 43 54 13 83
alain-lecomte.net
⊕ 11/N12

Galerie Meyer Oceanic Art
17 r des Beaux Arts, 6th
Ⓜ St-Germain-des-Prés
ⓒ 01 43 54 85 74
galerie-meyer-oceanic-art.com
⊕ 11/N12

Musée des Arts Derniers
28 r St Gilles, 3rd
Ⓜ Chemin Vert
ⓒ 01 44 49 95 70
art-z.net
⊕ 12/U11

Saint-Germain-des-Prés contemporary mix

Galerie Denise René
196 bd St-Germain, 7th
ⓂSt-Germain-des-Prés
ⓒ 01 42 22 77 57
deniserene.com
⊕ 11/N12

Galerie Kamel Mennour
60 r Mazarine, 6th
Ⓜ Odéon
ⓒ 01 56 24 03 63
galeriemennour.com
⊕ 11/N12

Galerie Loevenbruck
40 r de Seine, 6th
Ⓜ Mabillon
ⓒ 01 53 10 85 68
loevenbruck.com
⊕ 11/N12

**Galerie G-Philippe
et Nathalie Vallois**
36 r de Seine, 6th
Ⓜ Mabillon
ⓒ 01 46 34 61 07
gallerie-vallois.com
⊕ 10/L12

Galerie Lara Vincy
47 r de Seine, 6th
Ⓜ Mabillon
ⓒ 01 43 26 72 51
lara-vincy.com
⊕ 11/N12

Pièce Unique
4 r Jacques Callot, 6th
Ⓜ Odéon
ⓒ 01 43 26 54 58
galeriepieceunique.com
⊕ 11/N12

See page 9
to scan the
directory

COLLECTIONS
AND MUSEUMS

Musée du Quai Branly
37 quai Branly, 7th

Previous page: Musée du Petit Palais
Avenue Winston Churchill, 8th

Paris offers an unrivalled array of major art collections and museums, often in splendid settings. But alongside the Louvre and the Centre Pompidou sit smaller, lesser known but equally enthralling specialist museums that display anything from tribal art to soup tureens.

03

Historic art collections

The colossal **Musée du Louvre** remains an inexhaustible source of interest, scanning ancient Egypt, Greek, Roman and Oriental antiquities, and unmissables of Western art, from Da Vinci's *Mona Lisa* to Géricault's *The Raft of the Medusa*. Meanwhile, the Manets, Monets, Renoirs and Degas at **Musée d'Orsay** read like a greatest hits of Impressionist painting, without forgetting earlier Realists (including Courbet's still shocking *L'Origine du Monde*) and Symbolists, substantial arrays of Gauguin, Cézanne, Van Gogh, the Nabis and Art Nouveau furniture. Recapture the Gothic spirit amid tapestries, Limoges enamels and sculpture at the glorious **Musée National du Moyen-Age**.

The **Musée National de l'Orangerie** has been brilliantly renovated, bringing natural light back into the oval rooms containing Monet's curved panorama of waterlilies in a pond, *Les Nymphéas*, while new basement galleries are testimony to the taste of collector-dealer Paul Guillaume, who snapped up masterpieces by the Douanier Rousseau, Renoir, Soutine and Cézanne. More Monets at **Musée Marmottan-Claude Monet** include *Impression Soleil Levant*, which gave its name to the movement; other Impressionists shown here include Caillebotte, Pissarro and Berthe Morisot.

Although often visited for temporary exhibitions, the eclectic municipal art collection in the **Musée du Petit Palais** is strong on the 19th and early 20th centuries. Maillol's sculptures and less-known early Nabis-period paintings are the focus of the **Musée Maillol-Fondation Dina Vierny**, founded by his muse and model, Vierny, whose collection of drawings by Matisse and Picasso, naive art and multiples by Duchamp is also on show.

Modern & contemporary art

If you enjoy contemporary art, head straight for the **Centre Pompidou**, whose collection is rivalled only by that of the Museum of Modern Art in New York. Although only a tiny proportion can ever be shown at one time, it features art from 1905 to the present, including substantial holdings of Picasso, Matisse, Braque, the Surrealists, *arte povera*, *nouveau réalisme* and Pop art.

The municipal collection of modern art at the **Musée d'Art Moderne de la Ville de Paris** focuses on French art, notably Cubists, the Ecole de Paris, Arp and Fautrier, plus international contemporary artists, such as Richter, Schutte and Douglas Gordon. Excellent temporary exhibitions tend to alternate between big modern shows and adventurous contemporary ones.

In 2005, Paris saw the arrival of the **MAC/VAL** (Musée d'Art Contemporain du Val de Marne), curiously the first permanent museum of contemporary art in the suburbs. Its low-slung cubist building houses a broadly thematic survey of French art since the 1950s, including Raynaud, Morellet, Raysse, Hains, Boltanski and a representative selection from the current scene.

03

Contemporary creation and exhibition spaces

The other principal institutions for contemporary art put on temporary exhibitions but don't have permanent collections. The **Palais de Tokyo Site de Création Contemporaine** lives up to its premise as a laboratory for contemporary art, reactive to trends and events, and drawing a wide audience with its late hours. **Le Plateau** shares its gallery with the FRAC Ile-de-France, and though limited by lack of space, has been the place to discover heterogenous talents, such as Loris Gréaud and Adel Abdessemed. **La Laboratoire**, located

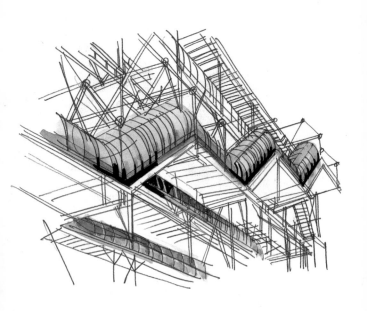

Centre Pompidou
rue Saint-Martin, 4th

in an old printworks near Palais Royal, aims to encourage new forms of creativity by exchanges between artists and scientists. Paris's only space devoted to naive or outsider art is **La Halle Saint-Pierre** in Montmartre.

Several French companies run independent spaces, of which **Fondation d'Entreprise Ricard** is the most adventurous. Its largely installation- or video-based shows include an annual exhibition of young artists leading to the Prix Ricard. **Fondation Cartier** puts on often striking exhibitions, accompanied by Thursday's Nomadic Nights performance season. Shows at the state electricity board's **Espace EDF-Electra** sometimes have a link to electricity. Shows at **Espace Louis Vuitton**, above the Vuitton flagship store, have ranged from Vanessa Beecroft to emerging Indian art, providing a look ahead at the future Fondation Vuitton, to be designed by iconoclastic architect Frank Gehry.

Crowd-pulling blockbuster shows are staged at the **Galeries Nationales du Grand Palais**, with smaller yet chic exhibitions at the **Musée du Luxembourg** and the independently run **Pinacothèque de Paris**.

The collector's eye

Welcome proof that private initiatives can succeed alongside the heavy hand of the state is provided by

La Maison Rouge, founded by collector Antoine de Galbert, which gives the chance to appreciate the vision of the solo connoisseur in rarely seen private collections. Other normally discreet collectors are also slowly coming out of the woodwork. The **Kadist Art Foundation**, opened in 2006 in Montmartre, and the **Fondation d'Art Contemporain Daniel et Florence Guerlain**, located in the Ile de France, puts on three exhibitions a year of works from private collections.

One-man shows

Visiting artists former homes and studios can provide an insight into their creative process. Most gloriously eccentric is the **Musée Gustave Moreau**, conceived by the Symbolist artist himself, with hundreds of his obsessive paintings crammed into the double-height studio where he worked. The **Musée Bourdelle** presents the oeuvre of sculptor Antoine Bourdelle, such as the frieze of the Théâtre des Champs-Elysées, and gives a vision of artistic Montparnasse of the early 20th century, through the perfectly preserved studios of Bourdelle and his neighbour, Eugène Carrière. Another relic of old Montparnasse is the home, now **Musée Zadkine**, of Russian emigré Ossip Zadkine, whose Cubist sculptures are dotted around the house and garden. The Atelier Brancusi was reconstructed outside the Centre Pompidou to look as it did when Constantin Brancusi worked in it, with his endless columns, tools, bed and photos. At **Musée Rodin**, in the 18th-century mansion where Rodin lived from 1908 to 1917, you can see *The Burghers of Calais*, *The Thinker* and *Gates of Hell* in the garden, while hundreds of portraits and studies, plus works by Camille Claudel are inside the house.

Picasso never lived at the beautiful Hôtel Salé, now the **Musée National Picasso**, but it does contain the works he kept in his possession and bequeathed to the French state. The collection covers all his periods and includes some remarkable sculptures and ceramics.

03

Tribal & oriental art

Musée du Quai Branly – ex-President Chirac's pet project in an extravagantly baroque modern building designed by Jean Nouvel – gives a theatrical presentation to sculptures, musical instruments and ritual objects from Africa, Asia, Australasia and the Americas, though wavers between an artistic perspective and an anthropological one. Decidely un-primitive Japanese and Chinese ceramics, Indo-Pakistani sculpture and stunning Buddhist sculptures from Angkor Wat in Cambodia are highlights at **Musée Guimet**. More Chinese art, notably hundreds of terracotta tomb figures, can be found at **Musée Cernuschi**. African sculpture and ritual items are presented at **Musée Dapper**.

Bibliothèque Forney
Hôtel de Sens, 1 rue de Figuier, 4th

Photography exhibitions

The **Jeu de Paume**, formed from the merger of the Centre National de la Photographie and the historical collection of the Patrimoine Photographique, operates from two sites with shows ranging from photographic pioneers and photojournalism to contemporary artists, such as Michal Rovner and Pierre et Gilles. The **Maison Européenne de la Photographie** presents international photography since the late 1950s. A more recent arrival is the **Fondation Henri Cartier-Bresson**, founded in 2003 by the late photographer and his wife Martine Frank in a Montparnasse studio. Aspects of Cartier-Bresson's long career alternate with other photographers, including the winner of the Grand Prix International Henri Cartier-Bresson.

03

Decorative and graphic art

Musée des Arts Décoratifs, in a wing of the Louvre, has been reinvigorated by a nine-year refurb, highlighting design and craftsmanship from the Middle Ages to contemporary designers. Chronological galleries are interspersed by time capsule-like period rooms, while the thematic galleries make fascinating juxtapositions of objects from different epochs. The building also contains the **Musée de la Mode et du Textile**, with shows about fashion, and **Musée de la Publicité**, about advertising. Posters, packaging and promotional

Musée des Arts Décoratifs, de la Publicité, de la Mode et du Textile
Palais du Louvre, 107 rue de Rivoli, 1st

memorabilia also feature at the **Bibliothèque Forney**. The **Musée de la Chasse et de la Nature** goes beyond the expected animal trophies and firearms to luscious paintings and decorative art, and an astonishing owl-feather ceiling by Belgian maverick Jan Fabre.

Architecture and design

Sprawling across the eastern wing of the Palais de Chaillot, the vast **Cité de l'Architecture** takes a two-pronged approach, on one hand presenting today's architecture to professionals and the general public, on the other touring French architectural heritage from the 12th to 18th centuries via spectacular full-scale plaster casts. The **Pavillon de l'Arsenal** follows Parisian urbanism, while the city's rich Modernist heritage can be explored at the **Fondation Le Corbusier**, two adjoining 1920s villas, where the celebrated architect first tried out some of his "Five Points of a New Architecture."

The foundation also administers **Le Corbusier's Flat** (open Wednesday morning only), where Le Corbusier and his wife lived for 30 years. Preserved just as when they lived here, it has an ingenious floor plan, magisterial open spiral staircase and cylindrical shower, and a play of colours and materials that is light years from the white box of Modernist's cliché.

03

Historic art collections

Musée Carnavalet
23 r de Sévigné, 3rd
Ⓜ St Paul
Ⓒ 01 44 59 58 58
parisfr/musees
✣ 11-12/T11

Musée Cognacq-Jay
8 r Elzévir, 3rd
Ⓜ St Paul
Ⓒ 01 40 27 07 21
paris.fr
✣ 10/l13

Musée Jacquemart-André
158 bd Haussmann, 8th
Ⓜ Miromesnil
Ⓒ 01 45 62 11 59
musee-jacquemart-andre.com
✣ 2-6/I5

Musée du Louvre
99 r de Rivoli, 1st
Ⓜ Palais Royal
Ⓒ 01 40 20 53 17
louvre.fr
✣ 6/M9

Musée du Luxembourg
19 r de Vaugirard, 6th
Ⓜ St Sulpice
Ⓒ 01 42 34 25 95
museeduluxembourg.fr
✣ 10-14/M14

**Musée Maillol -
Fondation Dina Vierny**
61 r de Grenelle, 7th
Ⓜ Rue du Bac
Ⓒ 01 42 22 59 50
museemaillol.fr
✣ 10/L13

**Musée Marmottan-
Claude Monet**
2 r Louis Boilly, 16th
Ⓜ Ranelagh
Ⓒ 01 44 96 50 33
marmottan.com
✣ Off map

**Musée National
du Moyen-Age**
6 pl Paul Painlevé, 5th
Ⓜ Cluny La Sorbonne
Ⓒ 01 53 73 78 00
musee-moyenage.fr
✣ 11-15/P14

**Musée National de
l'Orangerie**
Jardin des Tuileries, 1st
Ⓜ Concorde
Ⓒ 01 40 20 67 71
musee-orangerie.fr
✣ 6/L9

Musée d'Orsay
1 r de la Légion d'Honneur, 7th
Ⓜ Solférino
Ⓡ Musée d'Orsay
Ⓒ 01 40 49 48 14
musee-orsay.fr
✣ 10/K10

Musée du Petit Palais
av Winston Churchill, 8th
Ⓜ Champs-Elysées
Clemenceau
Ⓒ 01 53 43 40 00
petitpalais.paris.fr
✣ 6/H8

Pinacothèque de Paris
28 pl de la Madeleine, 8th
Ⓜ Madeleine
Ⓒ 01 42 68 02 01
pinacotheque.com
✣ 6/K7

The collector's eye

**Fondation d'Art
Contemporain Daniel et
Florence Guerlain**
5 r de la Vallée, 78490 Les
Mesnuls
Ⓒ 01 34 86 19 19
✣ Off map

Kadist Art Foundation
19 bis r des Trois Frères, 18th
Ⓜ Abbesses
Ⓒ 01 42 51 83 49
kadist.org
✣ 3/O2

La Maison Rouge
10 bd de la Bastille, 12th
Ⓜ Bastille
Ⓒ 01 40 01 08 81
lamaisonrouge.org
✣ 12/U12

Modern & contemporary art

Centre Pompidou
r St Martin, 4th
Ⓜ Rambuteau
Ⓣ 01 44 78 12 33
centrepompidou.fr
⊕ 7/R9

MAC/VAL
Carrefour de la Libération,
94400 Vitry sur Seine
Ⓜ Porte de Choisy, then
bus 183
Ⓣ 01 43 91 64 20
macval.fr
⊕ Off map

**Musée d'Art Moderne
de la Ville de Paris**
11 av du Président
Wilson, 16th
Ⓜ Alma Marceau
Ⓣ 01 53 67 40 00
mam.paris.fr
⊕ 5/D9

One-man shows

03

Espace Dali
11 r Poulbot, 18th
Ⓜ Abbesses
Ⓣ 01 42 64 40 10
daliparis.com
⊕ Off map

**Musée Départemental
Maurice Denis - Le Prieuré**
2bis r Maurice Denis,
78100 St Germain en Laye
ⓇⒺⓇ A St Germain en Laye
Ⓣ 01 39 73 77 87
musee-mauricedenis.fr
⊕ Off map

Musée National Picasso
Hôtel Salé,
5 r de Thorigny, 3rd
Ⓜ St Sébastien Froissart
Ⓣ 01 42 71 25 21
musee-picasso.fr
⊕ 10/J10

Fondation Arp
21 r des Châtaigniers,
Clamart
ⓇⒺⓇ C Meudon Val Fleury
Ⓣ 01 45 34 22 63
fondationarp.org
⊕ Off map

Musée Gustave Moreau
14 r de la Rochefoucauld,
9th
Ⓜ Trinité
Ⓣ 01 48 74 38 50
musee-moreau.fr
⊕ 2/M4

Musée Rodin
Hôtel Biron, 77 r de
Varenne, 7th
Ⓜ Varenne
Ⓣ 01 44 18 61 10
musee-rodin.fr
⊕ 10/I12

Musée Bourdelle
18 r Antoine Bourdelle, 15th
Ⓜ Falguière
Ⓣ 01 49 54 73 73
paris.fr/musees
⊕ 14/I16

**Musée National
Delacroix**
6 r Furstenberg, 6th
Ⓜ St-Germain-des-Prés
Ⓣ 01 44 41 86 50
musee-delacroix.fr
⊕ 11/N12

Musée Zadkine
100 bis r d'Assas, 6th
Ⓜ Notre Dame des Champs
Ⓣ 01 55 42 77 20
zadkine.paris.fr
⊕ 14 M16

Tribal & oriental art

Institut du Monde Arabe
1 r des Fossés St Bernard, 5th
Ⓜ Jussieu
Ⓒ 01 40 51 38 38
imarabe.org
⊕ 11-15/R14

Musée Cernuschi
7 av Vélasquez, 8th
Ⓜ Monceau
Ⓒ 01 53 96 21 50
paris.fr/musees/cernuschi
⊕ 2/H3

Musée Dapper
35 r Paul Valéry, 16th
Ⓜ Victor Hugo
Ⓒ 01 45 00 91 75
dapper.com
⊕ 5/C7

Musée Guimet
6 pl d'Iéna, 16th
Ⓜ Iéna
Ⓒ 01 56 52 53 00
museeguimet.fr
⊕ 5/D9

Musée du Quai Branly
37 quai Branly, 7th
Ⓜ Alma Marceau
ⓇⒺⓇ Pont de l'Alma
Ⓒ 01 56 61 72 72
quaibranly.fr
⊕ 9/E10

Panthéon Bouddhique
19 av de l'Iéna, 16th
Ⓜ Iéna
Ⓒ 01 40 73 88 00
museeguimet.fr
⊕ 5/D8

Decorative & graphic art

Bibliothèque Forney
Hôtel de Sens,
1 r de Figuier, 4th
Ⓜ St Paul
Ⓒ 01 42 78 14 60
paris.fr
⊕ 11/S12

Galerie Musée Baccarat
11 pl des Etats-Unis, 16th
Ⓜ Iéna
Ⓒ 01 40 22 11 00
baccarat.fr
⊕ 5/D7

**Musée d'Art et
d'Histoire du Judaïsme**
Hôtel de St Aignan,
71 r du Temple, 3rd
Ⓜ Rambuteau
Ⓒ 01 53 01 86 60
mahj.org
⊕ 11/R10

**Musée des Arts Décora-
tifs, de la Publicité,
de la Mode et du Textile**
Musée du Louvre,
107 r de Rivoli, 1st
Ⓜ Palais Royal
Ⓒ 01 44 55 57 60
lesartsdecoratifs.fr
⊕ 6/M9

**Musée de la Chasse
et de la Nature**
62 r des Archives, 3rd
Ⓜ Rambuteau
Ⓒ 01 53 01 92 40
chassenature.org
⊕ 11/S10

**Musée Nissim
de Camondo**
63 r de Monceau, 8th
Ⓜ Villiers
Ⓒ 01 53 89 06 50
lesartsdecoratifs.fr
⊕ 2/H4

Photography exhibitions

Fondation Henri Cartier-Bresson
2 impasse Lebouis, 14th
Ⓜ Edgar Quinet
Ⓒ 01 56 80 27 00
henricartierbresson.org
⊕ 14/K17

Jeu de Paume - Site Concorde
1 pl de la Concorde, 8th
Ⓜ Concorde
Ⓒ 01 47 03 12 50
jeudepaume.org
⊕ 6/J8

Maison Européenne de la Photographie
5 r de Fourcy, 4th
Ⓜ St Paul
Ⓒ 01 44 78 75 00
mep-fr.org
⊕ 11/S12

Architecture and design

Atelier Louis Barillet
15 sq de Vergennes, 15th
Ⓜ Vaugirard
Ⓒ 01 56 23 00 22
15squaredevergennes.com
⊕ 13/E17

Le Corbusier's Flat
24 r Nungesser et Coli, 16th
Ⓜ Michel Ange Molitor
Ⓒ 01 42 88 75 72
fondationlecorbusier.
asso.fr
⊕ Off map

Musée des Années Trente 03
28 av André Morizet,
92100 Boulogne
Billancourt
Ⓜ Marcel Sembat
Ⓒ 01 55 18 46 42
annees30.com
⊕ Off map

Cité de l'Architecture
45 av du Président-
Wilson, 16th
Ⓜ Trocadéro
Ⓒ 01 58 51 52 00
citechaillot.fr
⊕ 5/C9

Fondation Le Corbusier
Villa La Roche, 8-10 sq
du Dr Blanche, 16th
Ⓜ Jasmin
Ⓒ 01 42 88 41 53
fondationlecorbusier.
asso.fr
⊕ Off map

Pavillon de l'Arsenal
21 bd Morland, 4th
Ⓜ Sully Morland
Ⓒ 01 42 76 33 97
pavillon-arsenal.com
⊕ 11-12/T14

Contemporary creation and exhibition spaces

Espace EDF Electra
6 r Récamier, 7th
Ⓜ Sèvres Babylone
Ⓒ 01 53 63 23 45
edf.fr
⊕ 10/L13

Espace Louis Vuitton
60 r de Bassano, 8th
Ⓜ George V
Ⓒ 01 53 57 52 03
louisvuitton.com
⊕ 5/E6

Fondation Cartier
261 bd Raspail, 14th
Ⓜ Raspail
Ⓒ 01 42 18 56 50
fondation.cartier.fr
⊕ 14/L17

Fondation Cartier
261 boulevard Raspail, 14th

Contemporary creation and exhibition spaces

Fondation d'Entreprise Ricard
9 r Royale, 8th
Ⓜ Concorde
Ⓒ 01 53 30 88 00
fondation-entreprise-
ricard.com
✛ 6/K7

Le Laboratoire
4 r du Bouloi, 4th
Ⓜ Palais Royal
lelaboratoire.org
✛ 7/O9

Passage du Désir
BETC Euro RSCG
85-87 r du Fbg St
Martin, 10th
Ⓜ Gare de l'Est
Ⓒ 01 56 41 39 95
✛ 3-4/T3

Galeries Nationales du Grand Palais
3 av du Général
Eisenhower, 8th
Ⓜ Champs Elysées
Clemenceau
Ⓒ 01 41 57 32 28
rmn.fr
✛ 6/H8

Musée du Luxembourg
19 r de Vaugirard, 6th
Ⓜ St Sulpice
Ⓒ 01 42 34 25 95
museeduluxembourg.fr
✛ 14/M14

Pinacothèque de Paris `03`
28 pl de la Madeleine, 8th
Ⓜ Madeleine
Ⓒ 01 42 68 02 01
pinacotheque.com
✛ 6/K7

Halle St Pierre
2 r Ronsard, 18th
Ⓜ Anvers
Ⓒ 01 42 58 72 89
hallesaintpierre.org
✛ 3/P1

Palais de Tokyo Site de Création Contemporaine
13 av du Président
Wilson, 16th
Ⓜ Iéna
Ⓒ 01 47 23 38 86
palaisdetokyo.com
✛ 5/C9

Le Plateau
pl Hannah Arendt, 19th
Ⓜ Buttes Chaumont
Ⓒ 01 53 19 84 10
fracidf-leplateau.com
✛ 4/Z4

See page 9
to scan the
directory

CINEMAS AND
MOVIE LOCATIONS

Le Panthéon

Previous page: Studio des Ursulines
10 rue des Ursulines, 5th

P aris has been in love with cinema ever since the Lumière brothers held the world's first paid public film screening on rue Scribe in 1895. The choice of films on show at any one time is extraordinary, from French *cinéma d'auteur* and the latest US blockbusters via cult golden oldies to obscure African films, many shown in their original language. Multiplexes have made an impact here, but are matched by a valiant bunch of independent arts cinemas. For information, reservations and clips of what's on or about to come out, tap into websites Allocine (www.allocine.fr) and Cinefil (www.cinefil.fr).

04

Art house heartland

The Latin Quarter remains the heartland of Paris's arts cinemas. The **Cinéma du Panthéon** celebrated its centenary in 2007 by refurbishing its auditorium and opening a tea room decorated by Catherine Deneuve. Nearby, the **Accatone** screens art movies with the accent on films by Pasolini, Fassbinder and Antonioni. **Les Trois Luxembourg** mixes recent movies with meet-the-director sessions, documentaries and debates, while the pretty, plush velvet **Studio des Ursulines** is devoted to children's films.

The Latin Quarter cinema spirit is embodied by rue Champollion, a narrow street squeezed between boulevard Saint-Michel and the Sorbonne, where three cinemas, **Le Champo**, **Le Reflet Médicis Logos** and the **Filmothèque Quartier Latin**, offer foreign obscurities, themed retrospectives and Hollywood comedies. Cinephiles congregate at Le Reflet café across the street. Le Champo is particularly known for its all-night sessions of three films followed by breakfast.

Further along the rue des Ecoles, **Action Ecoles** and **Le Grand Action** (plus **Action Christine** in Saint-Germain) champion golden oldies from Hollywood; Grand Action also shows silent movies with live musical accompaniment. **Espace Saint-Michel** takes a more political slant. **Studio Galande** has been screening *The Rocky Horror Picture Show* every Friday and Saturday night since 1980. Dress up for the event and bring water, rice and other props.

Art cinemas elsewhere

The 1930s **l'Arlequin** hosts cineclubs, film previews, a short film festival and the *Un Certain Regard* selection hot from Cannes each summer. Founded in the 1920s, **Max Linder Panorama** prides itself on high-quality images, made possible by a large curved screen and serious black seating (black so as not to reflect any light).

The **Cinéma des Cinéastes**, run by the Société Civile d'Auteurs Réalisateurs Producteurs filmmakers association, offers a mix of exclusive new releases and film festivals. Art Deco **Le Balzac** differentiates itself from its Champs-Elysées neighbours with one-off events like Sunday cinema brunches, silent movies with live piano and pre-film concerts on Saturday nights. For a giggle, check out Paris's last porn cinema: **Le Beverley** caters to the lib with special entertainment, including couples evenings and erotic poetry readings.

04

L'Entrepôt, a converted warehouse, digs out previously unreleased films and films from developing nations, and hosts monthly sessions with composers of film music, and the regular Ciné-Philo – a film followed by philosophy debate in the bar. You can also hire its café and screening rooms for private film shows.

Foreign film specialists

Foreign films shown in their original language ("VO" in screening ads) are par for the course in art cinemas. Venturing beyond the main film-making nations, **Images d'Ailleurs** is dedicated to foreign films, notably from Africa and Iran; **Le Latina** shows films from Spain, Portugal, Latin America and Romania, and has a restaurant, gallery and tango lessons, while **Musée Guimet** is the place for such rarities as Afghan and Mongol films.

Musée Guimet
6 place d'Iéna, 16th

MK2 mix

Marin Karmitz's **MK2** chain is a clever halfway house between the mainstream giants and independent art houses. The small **MK2 Beaubourg** makes use of its site near the Centre Pompidou for a crossover art programme. At **MK2 Hautefeuille** regular events include "Raconte-moi un court," a mix of short films and poetry. **MK2 Quai de Seine** and **MK2 Quai de Loire** on either side of the Bassin de la Villette at Stalingrad have become a genuine local rendez-vous with their canal-side restaurants and a tiny ferry called *Zéro de Conduite* to convey you between the two.

04

Karmitz's take on the multiplex is the Jean-Michel Wilmotte-designed **MK2 Bibliothèque**, a triangular wedge next to the national library in new-look southeast Paris, with 14 cinemas, a café, three restaurants, DVD shop and bookstore. This is where Karmitz introduced the Martin Szekely-designed double cinema seat, a modern design response to the loveseat of old.

Commercial cinematics

Like any other city, Paris has its share of multiplexes. UGC's flagship, the 19-screen **UGC Ciné Cité Les Halles** shows all foreign films in VO and sells over two million tickets a year, while **Gaumont Champs-Elysées** retains a touch of Champs-Elysées chic.

Screen stars

Les Etoiles du Rex, the brilliant backstage tour **Le Grand Rex** (available in English) pays homage to this Art Deco icon and the golden age of cinema, while offering a witty initiation into cinematic tricks of the trade. Automatic doors and mystery voices lead you into the manager's office, behind the screen and into the projection room, before launching into a whirlwind of special effects, sound effects, and a casting for *King Kong*.

Le Grand Rex
1 boulevard Poissonnière, 2nd

Some cinemas merit a visit just for the building. Most glamorous of the lot is **Le Grand Rex**, an Art Deco temple whose illuminated crown stands out like a beacon on the Grands Boulevards. Inaugurated in 1932, its main auditorium is now used for rock concerts as well as films, seating 2,650 amid a gigantic fantasy setting of minarets and palm trees under a starry sky.

La Pagode, an extraordinary replica of a Japanese pagoda, complete with carved wood, sculpted lions and lacquer panels, was built in 1895 by the owner of Bon Marché for his mistress. It was converted into a cinema in 1931 and has a lovely tea room and Japanese garden. **Studio 28** in Montmartre, which opened in 1928 with decor by Jean Cocteau, has gone down in history as the scene of a public riot in 1930 during a screening of Buñuel's *L'Age d'Or*.

04

The heavyweights of Paris's repertory cinema are the **Forum des Images**, the **Cinémathèque de Paris** and the **Centre Pompidou**. Buried in Les Halles, the municipally-run Forum des Images concentrates on films about Paris, from features and documentaries to old newsreels and ads, but also shows animation and runs themed seasons; there is even a festival of films made on

La Pagode
57 bis rue de Babylone, 7th

mobile phones. The cinemas at the Centre Pompidou have an eclectic reach, including retrospectives, the annual Cinéma du Réel documentary festival, films by artists, children's films and a festival of dance films.

Founded in 1936, the erudite Cinémathèque de Paris moved in 2005 to the Gehry-designed former American Center. Three cinemas host an impressive repertoire of restored silent movies, retrospectives, and an ongoing history of French film. The building also houses the cinema museum (a display taking in magic lantern cameras, Marilyn's dress from *The Seven Year Itch* and the robot from *Metropolis*), temporary exhibitions and the BiFi film reference library.

04

Paris on the screen

Half of all films made in France are shot in Paris, and more than 730 films were shot in the city in 2006, 97 of them feature films. These included Claude Berri's *Ensemble C'est Tout* (with Audrey Tautou and Guillaume Canet), Jan Kounen's *99 Francs* (based on Frédéric Beigbeder's exposé of the Parisian advertising world) and André Techiné's AIDS-era parable *Les Témoins*.

Every part of Paris has its bit of film history: the Louvre in 1926's silent ghost story *Belphegor*, through Patrice Chéreau's bloodthirsty *La Reine Margot* (1994)

Agnès Varda

In *Daguerréotypes* (1975), director Agnès Varda films the inhabitants and shopkeepers of rue Daguerre in the 14th *arrondissement*, the street where she has lived for over half a century. Through the haberdashery, the hardware store, the butcher, filmed in real time, Varda builds a tribute to the everyday and an intimate portrait of a street through the people who live there.

to the *Da Vinci Code* (2006); the Champs-Elysées and Montparnasse in Godard's *A bout de souffle* (1960), the Saint-Germain of Eric Rohmer and Bastille of Cédric Klapisch. The Eiffel Tower also appears in everything, from Philip Noiret's vertiginous climb in Louis Malle's *Zazie dans le métro* (1960) to Grace Jones leaping off it in the Bond movie *A View to a Kill* (1985).

Long before the whimsically nostalgic Amélie Poulain took to the streets of Montmartre (fans can visit Amélie's café, the Café des Deux Moulins at 15 rue Lépic, and the Arab grocer in rue des Trois Moulins), the clubs, cabarets and streets of Montmartre and sleazier Pigalle embodied the city of Jean-Pierre Melville in films such as *Bob le Flambeur* (1956), *Le Doulos* (1962) and *Un Flic* (1972). Melville had other favourite haunts: Gare d'Austerlitz, the Champs-Elysées and the Métro, where Alain Delon, as cool as ice assassin Jef Costello, shakes off the cops in *Le Samouraï* (1967).

04

Cinema chez vous

If viewing the locations isn't enough, you can buy into film history at specialist film poster and book shops, from **Affiche Ciné** in the 18th to **Galerie Ciné-Images** in the 7th. An excellent source of English-language DVD rentals is **Prime Time Vidéo** but for all countries and all genres, **Vidéosphere** has it in the can.

La Cinémathèque de Paris
51 rue de Bercy, 12th

Art house heartland

Accatone
20 r Cujas, 5th
(RER) Luxembourg
(t) 01 46 33 86 86
⊕ 15/O15

Action Christine
4 r Christine, 6th
(M) St Michel
(t) 01 43 29 11 30
actioncinemas.com
⊕ 11/O12

Action Ecoles
23 r des Ecoles, 5th
(M) Maubert Mutalité
(t) 01 43 29 79 89
actioncinemas.com
⊕ 11-15/Q14

Le Champo
51 r des Ecoles, 5th
(M) Cluny La Sorbonne
(t) 01 43 54 51 60
lechampo.com
⊕ 11-15/Q14

Cinéma du Panthéon
13 r Victor Cousin, 5th
(RER) Luxembourg
(t) 01 40 46 01 21
cinema.pantheon.free.fr
⊕ 15/O15

Espace St Michel
7 pl St Michel, 5th
(M) St Michel
(t) 01 44 07 20 49
cinemasaintmichel.free.fr
⊕ 11/P13

Filmothèque Quartier Latin
9 r Champollion, 5th
(M) Cluny La Sorbonne
(t) 01 43 26 84 65
⊕ 11-15/O14

Le Grand Action
5 r des Ecoles, 5th
(M) Cardinal Lemoine
(t) 01 43 54 47 62
legrandaction.com
⊕ 11-15/Q14

Le Reflet Médicis Logos
3 r Champollion, 5th
(M) Cluny La Sorbonne
(t) 01 43 54 42 34
⊕ 11-15/O14

Studio Galande
42 r Galande, 5th
(M) St Michel
(t) 01 43 54 72 71
studiogalande.fr
⊕ 11/P13

Studio des Ursulines
10 r des Ursulines, 5th
(RER) Luxembourg
(t) 01 56 81 15 20
studiodesursulines.com
⊕ 15/O16

Les Trois Luxembourg
67 r Monsieur le Prince, 6th
(RER) Luxembourg
(t) 08 92 68 93 25
lestroisluxembourg.com
⊕ 11-15/O14

04

Screen icons

Le Grand Rex
1 bd Poissonnière, 2nd
(M) Bonne Nouvelle
(t) 08 92 68 05 96
legrandrex.com
⊕ 7/P6

La Pagode
57 bis r de Babylone, 7th
(M) St François Xavier
(t) 01 45 55 48 48
⊕ 10/J13

Studio 28
10 r Tholozé, 18th
(M) Abbesses
(t) 01 46 06 36 07
cinemastudio28.com
⊕ 3/N1

Art cinemas elsewhere

L'Arlequin
76 r de Rennes, 6th
Ⓜ St Sulpice
ⓒ 01 45 44 28 80
🜨 10-14/L14

Le Beverley
14 r de la Ville Neuve, 2nd
Ⓜ Bonne Nouvelle
ⓒ 01 40 26 00 69
cinebeverley.com
🜨 7/Q7

L'Entrepôt
7-9 r Francis de Pressensé, 14th
Ⓜ Pernéty
ⓒ 01 45 40 07 50
lentrepot.fr
🜨 Off map

Le Balzac
1 r Balzac, 8th
Ⓜ George V
ⓒ 01 45 61 10 60
cinemabalzac.com
🜨 5/E6

Cinéma des Cinéastes
7 av de Clichy, 17th
Ⓜ Pl de Clichy
ⓒ 01 53 42 40 00
larp.fr
🜨 2/K1

Max Linder Panorama
24 bd Poissonnière, 9th
Ⓜ Grands Boulevards
ⓒ 08 92 68 50 52
maxlinder.com
🜨 7/P6

Foreign film specialists

Images d'Ailleurs
21 r de la Clef, 5th
Ⓜ Censier Daubenton
ⓒ 01 45 87 18 09
🜨 7/R7

Le Latina
20 r du Temple, 4th
Ⓜ Hôtel de Ville
ⓒ 01 42 78 47 86
lelatina.com
🜨 11/R10

Musée Guimet
6 pl d'Iéna, 16th
Ⓜ Iéna
ⓒ 01 56 52 53 00
museeguimet.fr
🜨 5/D9

MK2 mix

MK2 Beaubourg
50 r Rambuteau, 3rd
Ⓜ Rambuteau
ⓒ 08 92 69 84 84
mk2.fr
🜨 11/R10

MK2 Hautefeuille
7 r Hautefeuille, 6th
Ⓜ St-Michel
ⓒ 08 92 69 84 84
mk2.fr
🜨 11/O13

MK2 Quai de Loire
7 quai de la Loire, 19th
Ⓜ Stalingrad
ⓒ 08 92 69 84 84
mk2.fr
🜨 4/X1

MK2 Bibliothèque
128 av de France, 13th
Ⓜ Bibliothèque
ⓒ 08 92 69 84 84
mk2.fr
🜨 Off map

MK2 Nation
133 bd Diderot, 12th
Ⓜ Nation
ⓒ 08 92 69 84 84
mk2.fr
🜨 16/Z15

MK2 Quai de Seine
14 quai de la Seine, 19th
Ⓜ Stalingrad
ⓒ 08 92 69 84 84
mk2.fr
🜨 4/W1

Heavyweights

Centre Pompidou
pl Georges Pompidou, 4th
Ⓜ Rambuteau
Ⓒ 01 44 78 12 33
centrepompidou.fr
⊕ 11/R10

Cinémathèque de Paris
51 r de Bercy, 12th
Ⓜ Bercy
Ⓒ 01 71 19 33 33
cinematheque.fr
⊕ 16/X17

Forum des Images
Porte St Eustache, 1st
Ⓜ Les Halles
Ⓒ 01 44 76 63 00
forumdesimages.net
⊕ 7/P9

Cinema chez vous

Affiche Ciné
1 r des Roses, 18th
Ⓜ Marx Dormoy
Ⓒ 01 44 72 95 09
affiche-cine.com
⊕ Off map

Contacts
24 r de Colisée, 8th
Ⓜ St Philippe du Roule
01 43 59 17 71
medialibrairie.com
⊕ 6/H6

Prime Time Vidéo
24 r Mayet, 6th
Ⓜ Duroc
Ⓒ 01 40 56 33 44
prime-time.org
⊕ 14/J15

04

Ciné-Doc
45-53 passage Jouffroy, 9th
Ⓜ Richelieu Drouot
Ⓒ 01 48 24 71 36
cine-doc.com
⊕ 7/O6

Galerie Ciné-Images
68 r de Babylone, 7th
Ⓜ St François Xavier
Ⓒ 01 47 05 60 25
cine-images.com
⊕ 10/J13

Vidéosphere
105 bd St Michel, 5th
Ⓡ Luxembourg
Ⓒ 01 43 26 36 22
videosphere.fr
⊕ 15Q/N16

Commercial cinematics

Gaumont Chps Elysées Marignan/Ambassade
27 and 50 av des Champs Elysées, 8th
Ⓜ F D Roosevelt
cinemasgaumontpathe.com
⊕ 6/H7

UGC Ciné Cité Bercy
2 cour St Emilion, 12th
Ⓜ Cour St Emilion
Ⓒ 08 92 70 00 00
ugc.fr
⊕ Off map

UGC Ciné Cité Les Halles
Forum des Halles, 1st
Ⓡ Châtelet Les Halles
Ⓒ 08 92 70 00 00
ugc.fr
⊕ 11/P10

See page 9
to scan the
directory

BOOKISH PURSUITS
AND CITY SCRIBES

Eglise Saint-Germain-des-Prés

Previous page: L'Arbre à Lettres
2 rue Edouard-Quenu, 5th

France prides itself on being a literary nation, and Saint-Germain-des-Prés is its literary epicentre. True, many publishers have moved away, but prestigious Gallimard and numerous smaller publishing houses are still based here, along with antiquarian bookshops and the Académie Française, the austere policeman of the French language based in the Institut de France. Saint-Germain's cafés – rendezvous of Enlightenment philosophers in the 18th century, Surrealists in the 1920s and existentialists in the 1940s and 1950s – are still port of call for the young writers who make up much of the new literary scene, such as Florian Zeller, Alexandre Jardin, Justine Lévy or opinion-maker Frédéric Beigbeder.

05

Ex-pat writers in Paris

The literary avant-garde flourished in Paris between the wars, as America's Lost Generation found refuge in inexpensive hotels, cafés and the city's new jazz clubs. The legendary tea parties given by Gertrude Stein and Alice B. Toklas in their apartment at 6 rue du Fleurus were gathering places for the artistic and literary avant-garde, including Hemingway, Ezra Pound, Ford Madox Ford, Picasso and Matisse, among others.

The sense of freedom that was in the air during the 1920s meant that several works in English were published here that were too experimental to see the light of day in Britain or the United States at the time, most celebrated being James Joyce's *Ulysses*, published in 1922 by Sylvia Beach at Shakespeare & Co.

At much the same time, George Orwell was working as a dishwasher at the Hôtel Lotti, living in severe poverty in a seedy hotel in rue du Pot au Fer, near rue Mouffetard, experiences he later committed to paper in his memoir *Down and Out in Paris and London*.

Sex, drugs and the beat poets

In the 1950s, William Burroughs, Allen Ginsberg and UK-born writer and painter Brion Gysin lived in a no-star, no-name hotel on rue Gît le Coeur, dubbed "the Beat Hotel" and now the rather more comfortable Relais du Vieux Paris. *The Naked Lunch*, William Burroughs's tale of a heroin addict's fall in a journey from New York to Tangiers, begun in a Moroccan hotel, was finished in Paris and published by Maurice Girodias's notorious Olympia Press in 1959. Olympia's titles included sexually explicit literature, and its financial undoing was J. P. Donleavy's first novel, *The Ginger Man*. Donleavy objected to his book being published as part of a porn list and sued the company.

Occupying a unique position between the French and ex-pat literary scenes was Samuel Beckett. After working as a reader at the Ecole Normale Supérieure in the 1920s, he returned to settle in Paris in 1938. He wrote many of his plays in French and English versions, such as the ground-breaking *Waiting for Godot*, which premiered at the now defunct Théâtre de Babylone in 1953.

French-language bookshops

Paris abounds with bookshops, including worthwhile mini-chain **l'Arbre à Lettres**. **Fnac Forum des Halles** is the flagship of the French book, music and multimedia chain, while **Gibert Joseph** is a wide-ranging generalist with the university slant that befits its Latin Quarter location, an English-language fiction section, and the useful practice of arranging secondhand books alongside new ones. **La Hune** is a favourite with Saint-Germain literati, who come for its excellent selection of fiction, criticism, art and design, and late opening hours.

The large **Librairie de Paris** is strong on literature and social sciences, with a good selection from small publishers. **Librairie Gallimard**, the publisher's own bookshop, includes other editions as well as its own books. Travel writing and meet-the-author sessions feature along with guides and maps of even the most obscure destinations at **Ulysse** and **Librairie Itinéraires**.

05

Bouquinistes along the Seine, 5th

Antiquarian bookshops are particularly concentrated in the Latin Quarter and Saint-Germain-des-Prés, where you'll also find the much loved *Bouquinistes*, booksellers operating out of green wooden boxes along the Seine. Book collectors also gather at the book market held each weekend in the iron pavilions of the former meat market at the Parc Georges Brassens.

English-language bookshops

You either love or hate **Shakespeare & Co.**, named after (but independent of) Sylvia Beach's famous rue de l'Odéon store. It's always full of earnest young would-be writers and books are chaotically arranged, but it is a good place to meet literary-minded people. It opens daily until midnight and runs an active schedule of events: readings by authors most Monday evenings, travel writing weekends, and the Other Writers' Group Saturday afternoon workshop.

05

Village Voice Bookshop, run by Odette Hellier, is known for its good choice of mainly North American literature and meet-the-author readings by notables such as Toni Morrison, Richard Ford, Douglas Kennedy and Margaret Atwood. The **Red Wheelbarrow Bookshop**, in the Marais, has adults's and children's sections and a roster of readings and signings that includes French writers who have recently been translated into English,

Shakespeare & Co
37 rue de la Bûcherie, 5th

A Parisian puzzle

Georges Perec's *La Vie Mode d'Emploi* (translated as *Life a User's Manual*) is not merely a masterpiece of Oulipienne literature, constructed like a jigsaw puzzle or chess game, but also an exploration of that quintessentially Parisian form of accommodation, the Haussmannian apartment block. It navigates chapter by chapter geographically and across the decades from boiler room via bourgeois apartment to *chambre de bonne*, describing rooms, floors, staircase and the assorted lives contained within.

as well as English-language authors. The city's best general English-language bookstores are **W. H. Smith**, a superior century-old branch of the British chain, where a huge choice of fiction, non-fiction and reference books is supplemented by UK and US newspapers and magazines, and American bookstore **Brentano's**. **Galignani**, the oldest English-language bookshop in continental Europe, was a favourite with voyagers on the Grand Tour in the 1830s. Today it carries French as well as English literature and has an excellent art section.

For secondhand books, try the **San Francisco Book Co.**, whose content ranges from crime paperbacks to collectors's first editions, and the more homely **Tea & Tattered Pages**, a bookstore and tea room all in one.

05

Literary sightseeing

Visiting the **Maison de Victor Hugo**, the second-floor apartment on Place des Vosges where Hugo lived from 1832 to 1848, may not explain the writer's genius but does give you a vision of his complicated and sometimes tragic family life and his eclectic hobbies. Here you can see his red damask bedroom; the neo-medieval dining room furniture he designed for his mistress, Juliet Drouet, when in exile in Guernsey; her Chinese salon; and evidence of his interest in photography, with early daguerreotypes taken by Hugo and his sons.

Musée Carnavalet
23 rue de Sévigné, 3rd

Equally atmospheric are the creaky floorboards and narrow staircases of the **Maison de Balzac** in Passy, where Honoré de Balzac rented an apartment from 1840 to 1847, living as M. de Breugnol to avoid his creditors, and where he wrote many of the 100 or so novels and plays which form his oeuvre known as *La Comédie Humaine*. The display includes manuscripts and heavily annotated proofs, his coffee-pot, portraits, letters, and illustrations of his characters.

The letter-writing Marquise de Sévigné rented the beautiful Hôtel Carnavalet from 1677 to 1696. It is now part of **Musée Carnavalet**, where her portrait and lacquered desk can be seen among its eclectic collection devoted to Parisian history, as can Voltaire's chair and Proust's bedroom. George Sand didn't actually live at what is now the **Musée de la Vie Romantique** – she and her lover, the composer Frédéric Chopin, both had apartments at the nearby square d'Orléans – but she often attended salons here when it was the home of history painter and portraitist Ary Scheffer, and her letters, watercolours (she was a pupil and friend of Delacroix) and jewellery are among the mementoes. Another Romantic idyll is the **Maison de Chateaubriand** in the Vallée aux Loups, the 18th century country house and gardens transformed by the author of *Mémoires d'outre tombe*.

Musée de la Vie Romantique
16 rue Chaptal, 9th

Literary events

Readings and author signings take place in numerous bookshops. Among the most active are the **Espace Harmattan**, attached to the eponymous Latin Quarter publisher and bookshop, with a large list of authors from Arab and developing countries as well as social sciences, and **Librairie le Merle Moqueur**, which regularly puts on events on Sundays. The **Théâtre Mouffetard** runs an interesting series featuring works by winners of the Nobel Prize for Literature.

Poetry readings

Every spring poetry readings take place in cafés around Paris as part of the Printemps des Poètes festival. All year round, look out for events at the **Maison de la Poésie**, which aims to widen the audience for poetry through poetry readings and shows in the picturesque 18th century Théâtre Molière. A more convivial approach is taken by **Club des Poètes**, where poetry classics and works by young poets are performed by actors and singers in diverse *dîner-spectacles*.

English-language poetry gets a regular airing in John Klipham's **Live Poets Society**, which holds monthly readings by an impressive roster of new and established poets at the Highlander Pub.

05

French-language bookshops

L'Arbre à Lettres
33 r du bd du Temple, 3rd
Ⓜ République
ⓒ 01 48 04 76 52
⊕ 8/U8

L'Arbre à Lettres
2 r Edouard Quenu, 5th
Ⓜ Censier Daubenton
ⓒ 01 43 31 74 08
⊕ Off map

Fnac Forum des Halles
Forum des Halles, 1st
ⓇⒺⓇ Châtelet-Les-Halles
ⓒ 0825 020 020
fnac.com
⊕ 11/P10

Gibert Joseph
26 bd St-Michel, 5th
Ⓜ Cluny La Sorbonne
ⓒ 01 44 41 88 88
gibertjoseph.com
⊕ 11-15/O14

La Hune
170 bd St-Germain, 6th
Ⓜ St Germain des Prés
ⓒ 01 45 48 35 85
⊕ 10/L12

Librairie Gallimard
15 bd Raspail, 7th
Ⓜ Rue du Bac
ⓒ 01 45 48 24 84
librairie-gallimard.com
⊕ 10/K13

Librairie Itinéraires
60 r St-Honoré, 1st
Ⓜ Châtelet
ⓒ 01 42 36 12 63
itineraires.com
⊕ 11/O10

Librairie de Paris
7 pl de Clichy, 17th
Ⓜ Place de Clichy
ⓒ 01 45 22 47 81
librairie-de-paris.fr
⊕ 2/L2

Ulysse
26 r St-Louis-en-l'Ile, 4th
Ⓜ Pont Marie
ⓒ 01 43 25 17 35
ulysse.fr
⊕ 11/S13

Literary events

Espace Harmattan
21 bis r des Ecoles, 5th
Ⓜ Maubert Mutualité
ⓒ 01 40 46 79 10
editions-harmattan.fr
⊕ 15/Q15

Librairie le Merle Moqueur
51 r de Bagnolet, 20th
Ⓜ Alexandre Dumas
ⓒ 01 40 09 08 80
lemerlemoqueur.fr
⊕ Off map

Théâtre Mouffetard
73 r Mouffetard, 5th
Ⓜ Place Monge
ⓒ 01 45 35 31 15
theatremouffetard.com
⊕ 15/Q16

Poetry readings

Club des Poètes
30 r de Bourgogne, 7th
Ⓜ Varenne
ⓒ 01 47 05 06 03
poesie.net
⊕ 10/I11

Live Poets Society
The Highlander Pub,
8 r de Nevers, 6th
Ⓜ Odéon
ⓒ 01 43 26 54 20
the-highlander.fr
⊕ 11/N12

Maison de la Poésie
Passage Molière,
157 r St Martin, 3rd
Ⓜ Rambuteau
ⓒ 01 44 54 53 00
maisondelapoesieparis.com
⊕ 7/R9

Literary sightseeing

Maison de Balzac
47 r Raynouard, 16th
Ⓜ Passy
© 01 55 74 41 80
paris.fr/musees
⊕ Off map

Maison Chateaubriand
La Vallée aux Loups,
92290 Chatenay-
Malabry
Ⓡ Robinson
© 01 47 02 08 62
maison-de-chateaubriand.fr
⊕ Off map

Maison de Victor Hugo
6 pl des Vosges, 4th
Ⓜ Bastille
© 01 42 72 10 16
parisfr/musees
⊕ 12/U12

Musée Carnavalet
23 r de Sévigné, 3rd
Ⓜ St Paul
© 01 44 59 58 58
parisfr/musees
⊕ 11-12/T11

Musée Jean Cocteau
(opens spring 2008)
r de Lau, 91490
Milly-la-Forêt
jeancocteau.net
⊕ Off map

Musée de la Vie Romantique
16 r Chaptal, 9th
Ⓜ Blanche
© 01 53 31 95 67
parisfr/musees
⊕ 10/M13

English-language bookshops

05

Brentano's
37 av de l'Opéra, 2nd
Ⓜ Opéra
© 01 42 61 52 50
brentanos.fr
⊕ 6/M7

Galignani
224 r de Rivoli, 1st
Ⓜ Tuileries
© 01 42 60 76 07
⊕ 6/K8

NQL
78 bd St Michel, 6th
Ⓡ Luxembourg
© 01 43 26 42 70
⊕ 15/N16

Red Wheelbarrow Bookshop
22 r St Paul, 4th
Ⓜ St Paul
© 01 48 04 75 08
theredwheelbarrow.com
⊕ 11-12/T13

San Francisco Book Co
17 r Monsieur le Prince, 6th
Ⓜ Odéon
© 01 43 29 15 70
sanfranciscobooksparis.com
⊕ 11-15/ O14

Shakespeare & Co.
37 r de la Bûcherie, 5th
Ⓜ St Michel
© 01 43 25 40 93
shakespeareco.org
⊕ 11/P13

Tea & Tattered Pages
24 r Mayet, 6th
Ⓜ Duroc
© 01 40 65 94 35
teaandtatteredpages.com
⊕ 14/J15

Village Voice Bookshop
6 r Princesse, 6th
Ⓜ Mabillon
© 01 46 33 36 47
villagevoicebookshop.com
⊕ 10/M13

W. H. Smith
248 r de Rivoli, 1st
Ⓜ Concorde
© 01 44 77 88 99
whsmith.fr
⊕ 6/K8

See page 9
to scan the
directory

MUSIC AND THE
PERFORMING ARTS

Palais Garnier
place de l'Opéra, 9th

Previous page: Batofar
11 quai François-Mauriac, 13th

Whether you're after glorious operatic spectacle, laidback jazz, radical dance or an intellectual theatrical challenge, you will find plenty of opportunities to discover adventurous new creations in Paris's huge array of concert halls and theatres.

Classical music and opera

Few things can beat the glamour of a soirée at the opulent Palais Garnier, yet the **Opéra National de Paris**, directed by Gérard Mortier, offers some daring modern opera alongside predictable sellout hits. Productions are shared between Palais Garnier and its modern sibling, the Opéra Bastille, one of Mitterrand's most controversial *grands projets*. Major visiting opera companies and co-productions can also be found at the **Théâtre du Châtelet**, along with star piano soloists and a renowned Sunday-morning concert series.

06

The smaller **Opéra Comique** has an illustrious past as the place where Bizet's *Carmen* and Debussy's *Pelléas et Mélisande* were premiered. Director Jérôme Deschamps, famed creator with Macha Makeïeff of the inimitable Deschiens troupe, arrived for the 2007-

2008 season and is hoped to revive its artistic credibility with top-notch conductors and a roster of productions ranging from Baroque opera by Lully to modern opera by Pascal Dusapin. Tiny **Péniche Opéra** is an interesting alternative: a canal barge where young singers get the opportunity to perform in scaled-down operettas.

The **Maison de Radio France**, home of state radio broadcasting and responsible for the Orchestre National de France and the Orchestre Philharmonique de Radio France, puts on varied concerts in its own circular building and other concert halls. The Orchestre National de France also plays at the **Théâtre des Champs-Elysées**, which draws a dressy audience for vocal recitals, guest orchestras and gala dance productions. Meanwhile, the Orchestre Philharmonique de Radio France and the Orchestre de Paris are based at **Salle Pleyel**, reopened in 2006 after a four-year refurbishment that restored its Art Deco foyers and improved acoustics. The resident orchestras are joined by an array of illustrious visitors, such as the Berliner Philharmoniker, the London Symphony Orchestra and Europa Galante. The **Cité de la Musique** at La Villette puts on particularly diverse themed seasons, though for truly experimental work and sounds composed by computer, the place to go is **IRCAM**, the unique music research institute created by Pierre Boulez in the 1970s as an offshoot of the Centre Pompidou.

Jazz clubs

Jazz continues to be a Parisian passion, although Saint-Germain-des-Prés is no longer the focus, as the best clubs are now scattered throughout the city. Located on a scruffy sidestreet, the **New Morning** remains the cult address for big jazz, blues and Latino musicians. **Le Sunset** cellar club in Les Halles (with an upstairs acoustic offshoot, **Sunside**) celebrated its 25th anniversary in 2007 and has been responsible for introducing and supporting some major French talents, such as the brass-playing Belmondo brothers, pianist Laurent de Wilde and young saxophonist Sophie Alour.

Despite a business-hotel atmosphere, the **Jazz Club Lionel Hampton** is *the* place for top-quality traditional swing and big band sounds. At the other end of the scale, the tiny **Le Franc Pinot** wine bar is often used by radio station France Musiques for live jazz broadcasts. **Les Sept Lézards** jazz cellar is a favourite with local musicians, with free jam sessions on Sundays.

06

Rock and chanson

French singers seem to last for ever – eternal rocker Johnny Hallyday and crooner Alain Souchon look and sound much as they did 30 years ago. Even Sartre muse Juliette Gréco still makes an occasional appearance. Fortunately, there's also a worthwhile *nouvelle*

Café de la Danse
5 passage Louis-Philippe, 11th

chanson scene, where singer-songwriters like Jérôme Attal, Jeanne Balibar, Coralie Clément and the Suzanne Vega-ish Keren Ann take centre stage. The French Touch electronic scene lives on with Daft Punk, Air, Gotan Project's acclaimed mix of tango and electro, newcomers Justice, and IRCAM-trained Emilie Simon, who wrote the soundtrack to French film *La Marche de l'Empereur* (*The March of the Penguins*, 2005).

Paris's most illustrious venue is the **Olympia**, a plush vintage theatre, which holds a sentimental pull for perennial French stars and international comebacks, and marks the consecration of younger bands. Other rock bands and *chanson* acts play a series of old theatres and music halls, like **La Cigale** and **Le Bataclan**. The **Café de la Danse** is a good place to discover *nouvelle chanson*.

Berber, rai and gypsy music often feature in the atmospheric circus setting of the **Cabaret Sauvage** at La Villette. **La Maroquinerie** is mainly in rock mode, while trendy red lighthouse ship **Batofar** features new rock, electro and unusual crossovers. **Le Réservoir**, a former ironworks adorned with big baroque mirrors, is a music industry hangout and a good place for sounding out new talents, as is the spectacular **Le Showcase**, housed inside the ornate Pont Alexandre III, though it is reserved for private events during the week.

06

Théâtre National de Chaillot
1 place du Trocadéro, 16th

Ballet and contemporary dance

The enduring popular image of dance in Paris is the Degas-esque tutus of the Opéra National de Paris, but this contrasts with a dynamic, often challenging contemporary dance scene. Even at the Opéra National, the classical repertoire of works choreographed by Nureyev, Balanchine and Petipa is being tempered by choreographers such as South Africa's Robyn Orlin and Aix-en-Provence-based Angelin Preljocaj.

The temple for contemporary dance is the **Théâtre de la Ville**, where regular visits from cult international figures Pina Bausch, Meg Stuart, Maguy Marin and Gilles Jobin are inevitable sell-outs. At the massive 1930s **Théâtre National de Chaillot** and the innovative **Théâtre de la Bastille**, an exciting range of dance companies alternates with theatre productions. **Théâtre de la Cité Internationale** hosts visiting companies alongside works from resident choreographer-dancer Mark Tompkins, while **La Ménagerie de Verre** is daringly interdisciplinary; shows here often mix theatre, dance, music and visual art, notably in its springtime Etrange Cargo festival. It's also worth crossing the Périphérique to the **Centre National de la Danse**, a rehabilitated office block that serves as an umbrella group for France's hundreds of dance companies, with courses, seminars, archives and performances.

06

Comédie Française
Salle Richelieu
2 place Colette, 1st

Just for laughs

Shazia Mirza, Arthur Smith, Rich Hall and Greg Proops are just a few of the talents hot from the English and stateside comedy circuit who like to drop in for a few nights in Paris. **Laughing Matters** has now been programming English stand-up comedy in Paris for more than a decade, ever since promoter Karel Beer first brought Eddie Izzard over on the Eurostar in 1995. Shows take place at La Java (105 r du Faubourg du Temple, 10th; M° République; tel: 01 42 02 20 52, anythingmatters.com), an atmospheric old dance hall where Piaf once trod the boards.

Underground and multi-disciplinary

A more underground scene exists too. **Mains d'Oeuvres**, a rehabilitated factory social club, and **Point Ephémère**, a canalside warehouse, have a more offbeat grungy feel, combining concert venue, performance spaces, bar-restaurant and art gallery. Laidback **Glazart**, an old coach station, features concerts, club nights, video projections, and an outside terrace for sunbathing, skittles and *pétanque* in summer.

Theatre and stage productions

The most innovative productions tend to be put on at the state-supported public theatres in Paris and the suburbs, while the big private theatres usually stick to more mainstream fare and comedies. The **Comédie Française**, administered by its member actors or *pensionnaires*, is France's oldest theatre company. Molière remains the backbone of its repertoire, although more recent international playwrights are often staged at its **Vieux-Colombier** space and new works get an airing at its **Studio Théâtre**.

06

More experimental work can be found at Ariane Mnouchkine's **Théâtre du Soleil**. Many pieces are created by the company as a collective, while others result from Mnouchkine's collaborations with writer Hélène Cixous. It is just one of six interesting theatres

Théâtre des Champs-Elysées
15 avenue Montaigne, 8th

at the **Cartoucherie de Vincennes,** a former match factory in the Bois de Vincennes, along with the **Théâtre de la Tempête** and the **Théâtre de l'Aquarium**.

Another legendary address is Peter Brook's **Théâtre Les Bouffes du Nord**, at its best in productions staged by the veteran British director himself. Brook often works with the same faithful group of actors and draws devoted fans to this once-abandoned theatre, where he has preserved an artfully distressed aesthetic of peeling paint and punishingly hard seats. The **Théâtre National de la Colline** focuses on modern European authors, notably Thomas Bernhard and Edward Bond, many of whose plays have had their world premieres here, directed by Alain Franchon. A European repertoire from ancient Greece to the present also features in the often-acclaimed productions at the **Théâtre de l'Odéon**, performed in its beautiful 18th century main house in Saint-Germain, as well as the warehouse-style Ateliers Berthier in the 17th *arrondissement*. Pigalle's **Théâtre Ouvert** is dedicated to producing and publishing new, often politically engaged, texts, along with workshops, readings and encounters with playwrights.

06

Paris has hundreds of private theatres ranging from big boulevard venues like the **Théâtre de la Porte Saint Martin**, **Théâtre Edouard VII** and glamorous Second

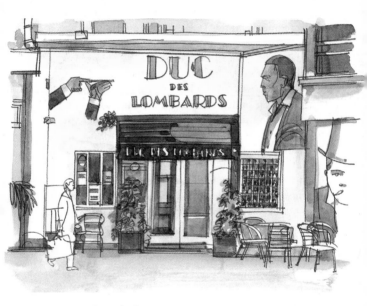

Le Duc des Lombards
42 rue des Lombards, 1st

Empire **Théâtre Marigny** to tiny fringe venues putting on drama, comedy and one-man shows. A place apart belongs to the **Théâtre de la Huchette**, where Nicolas Bataille's production of Ionescu's absurdist *La Cantatrice Chauve* has been playing without a break and with some of the same cast since its premiere in 1948.

If it's plush velvet, gilding and backstage stories that interest you more than what's on the stage, then it might be worth taking one of **Agence Purple Beam's** behind-the-scenes tours of some of the city's prettiest historic theatres, such as the Théâtre des Variétés, Théâtre Marigny, the Théâtre de la Porte-Saint-Martin and the Opéra Comique. The agency does tours in various languages for groups, and visits for individuals in French.

06

Theatre in English

A number of small Paris-based companies, such as the On Stage Theatre Co., put on English-language productions in small theatres around Paris. Look also for innovative theatre companies such as New York's Wooster Group and the UK's Forced Entertainment which regularly crop up at the Centre Pompidou or during the Festival d'Automne. Occasional visits by the Royal Shakespeare Company, generally to the Théâtre National de Chaillot, and Declan Donnellan's Cheek by Jowl company are also well worth investigating.

Ballet and contemporary dance

**Centre National
de la Danse**
1 r Victor Hugo,
93507 Pantin
Ⓜ Hoche
Ⓒ 01 41 83 27 27
cnd.fr
⊕ Off map

La Ménagerie de Verre
12-14 r Léchevin, 11th
Ⓜ Parmentier
Ⓒ 01 43 38 33 44
menagerie-de-verre.org
⊕ 8/W9

Théâtre de la Bastille
76 r de la Roquette, 11th
Ⓜ Bastille
Ⓒ 01 43 57 42 14
theatre-bastille.com
⊕ 12/W12

**Théâtre de la Cité
Internationale**
17 bd Jourdan, 14th
ⓇⒺⓇ Cité Universitaire
Ⓒ 01 43 13 50 50
theatredelacite.com
⊕ Off map

**Théâtre National
de Chaillot**
1 pl du Trocadéro, 16th
Ⓜ Trocadéro
Ⓒ 01 53 65 30 00
theatre-chaillot.fr
⊕ 5/B9

Théâtre de la Ville
2 pl du Châtelet, 4th
Ⓜ Châtelet
Ⓒ 01 42 74 22 77
theatredelaville-paris.com
⊕ 11/P11

Rock and chanson

Le Bataclan
50 bd Voltaire, 11th
Ⓜ Voltaire
Ⓒ 01 43 14 00 30
le-bataclan.com
⊕ 12/Y12

Batofar
11 quai François-Mauriac,
13th
Ⓜ Bibliothèque
Ⓒ 01 53 60 17 30
batofar.org
⊕ Off map

Cabaret Sauvage
Parc de la Villette,
59 bd MacDonald, 19th
Ⓜ Porte de la Villette
Ⓒ 01 42 09 01 09
cabaretsauvage.com
⊕ Off map

Café de la Danse
5 passage Louis-Philippe,
11th
Ⓜ Bastille
Ⓒ 01 47 00 57 59
cafedeladanse.com
⊕ 12/W12

La Cigale/La Boule Noire
120 bd Rochechouart, 18th
Ⓜ Anvers
Ⓒ 01 55 07 06 00
lacigale.fr
⊕ 3/P2

La Maroquinerie
23 r Boyer, 20th
Ⓜ Gambetta
Ⓒ 01 40 33 35 05
lamaroquinerie.fr
⊕ Off map

Olympia
28 bd des Capucines, 9th
Ⓜ Opéra
Ⓒ 01 55 27 10 00
olympiahall.com
⊕ 6/L7

Le Réservoir
16 r de la Forge Royale, 11th
Ⓜ Ledru Rollin
Ⓒ 01 43 56 39 60
reservoirclub.com
⊕ 12/X13

Le Showcase
Under Pont Alexandre III
(Right Bank), 8th
Ⓜ Invalides
Ⓒ 01 45 61 25 43
showcase.fr
⊕ 6/H9

Classical music and opera

Auditorium du Louvre
Musée du Louvre, 1st
Ⓜ Palais Royal
℃ 01 40 20 55 00
louvre.fr
✛ 11/N10

Cité de la Musique
221 av Jean Jaurès, 19th
Ⓜ Porte de Pantin
℃ 01 44 84 44 84
cite-musique.fr
✛ Off map

IRCAM
1 pl Igor Stravinsky, 4th
Ⓜ Hôtel de Ville
℃ 01 44 78 48 43
ircam.fr
✛ 11/Q10

Maison de Radio France
116 av du Président-
Kennedy, 16th
Ⓜ Kennedy-Radio France
℃ 01 56 40 15 16
radiofrance.fr
✛ 9/A12

Opéra Comique
pl Boïeldieu, 2nd
Ⓜ Richelieu Drouot
℃ 01 42 44 45 40
opera-comique.com
✛ 6/M6

Opéra National de Paris
Palais Garnier
pl de l'Opéra, 9th
Ⓜ Opéra
℃ 08 92 89 90 90
www.operadeparis.fr
✛ 6/M6

Opéra National de Paris
Opéra Bastille
pl de la Bastille, 12th
Ⓜ Bastille
℃ 08 92 89 90 90
www.operadeparis.fr
✛ 12/V13

Péniche Opéra
Opposite 46 quai de
Loire, 19th
Ⓜ Jaurès
℃ 01 53 35 07 77
penicheopera.com
✛ 4/X1

Salle Gaveau
45 r La Boétie, 8th
Ⓜ Miromesnil
℃ 01 49 53 05 07
sallegaveau.com
✛ 6/H6

Salle Pleyel
252 r du Fbg St-Honoré,
8th
Ⓜ Ternes
℃ 01 42 56 13 13
sallepleyel.fr
✛ 1-5/F5

Théâtre des Champs Elysées
15 av Montaigne, 8th
Ⓜ Alma Marceau
℃ 01 49 52 20 20
theatrechampselysees.fr
✛ 5/F8

Théâtre du Châtelet
1 pl du Châtelet, 1st
Ⓜ Châtelet
℃ 01 40 28 28 00
chatelet-theatre.com
✛ 11/P11

06

Jazz clubs

Le Duc des Lombards
42 r des Lombards, 1st
Ⓜ Châtelet Les Halles
Ⓣ 01 42 33 22 88
ducdeslombards.fr
⊕ 11/P10

Jazz Club Lionel Hampton
81 bd Gouvion St Cyr, 17th
Ⓜ Porte Maillot
Ⓣ 01 40 68 30 42
jazzclub-paris.com
⊕ 1/B3

Les Sept Lézards
10 r des Rosiers, 4th
Ⓜ St Paul
Ⓣ 01 48 87 08 97
7lezards.com
⊕ 11/S11

Le Franc Pinot
1 quai de Bourbon, 4th
Ⓜ Pont Marie
Ⓣ 01 46 33 60 64
franc-pinot.com
⊕ 11/R13

New Morning   ·
7-9 r des Petites Ecuries, 10th
Ⓜ Gare de l'Est
Ⓣ 01 45 23 51 41
newmorning.com
⊕ 7/Q5

Le Sunset/Sunside
60 r des Lombards, 1st
Ⓜ Châtelet Les Halles
Ⓣ 01 40 26 46 60
sunset-sunside.com
⊕ 11/P1O

Multi-disciplinary alternatives

Glazart
7-15 av de la Porte de la
Villette, 19th
Ⓜ Porte de la Villette
Ⓣ 01 40 36 55 65
glazart.com
⊕ Off map

Mains d'Oeuvres
1 r Charles Garnier,
93400 St Ouen
Ⓜ Porte de Clignancourt.
Ⓣ 01 40 11 25 25.
mainsdoeuvres.org
⊕ Off map

Point Ephémère
200 quai de Valmy, 10th
Ⓜ Stalingrad
Ⓣ 01 40 34 02 48
pointephemere.org
⊕ 4/U3

Theatre and stage productions

Agence Purple Beam
33 r Le Peletier, 9th
Ⓜ Le Peletier
Ⓣ 01 41 10 08 10
purplebeam.com
⊕ 7/N6

**Comédie Française
Studio Théâtre**
Carrousel du Louvre, 1st
Ⓜ Palais Royal
Ⓣ 01 44 58 98 58
comedie-francaise.fr
⊕ 10/M10

**Comédie Française
Salle Richelieu**
2 pl Colette, 1st
Ⓜ Palais Royal
Ⓣ 08 25 10 16 80
comedie-francaise.fr
⊕ 7/N9

Comédie Française Théâtre du Vieux Colombier
21 r du Vieux Colombier, 6th
Ⓜ St Sulpice
Ⓒ 01 44 39 87 00
comedie-francaise.fr
⊕ 10/M13

Théâtre de l'Aquarium
route du Champ de Manoeuvre, 12th
Ⓜ Château de Vincennes + shuttle bus
Ⓒ 01 43 74 99 61
theatredelaquarium.com
⊕ Off map

Théâtre des Bouffes du Nord
37 bis bd de la Chapelle, 10th
Ⓜ La Chapelle
Ⓒ 01 46 07 34 50
bouffesdunord.com
⊕ 3-4/T2

Théâtre Edouard VII
10 pl Edouard VII, 9th
Ⓜ Opéra
Ⓒ 01 47 42 35 71
theatreedouard7.com
⊕ 6/L6

Théâtre de la Huchette
23 r de la Huchette, 5th
Ⓜ St Michel
Ⓒ 01 43 26 38 99
theatrehuchette.com
⊕ 11/P13

Théâtre Marigny
av de Marigny, 8th
Ⓜ Champs-Elysées Clémenceau
Ⓒ 01 53 96 70 30
theatremarigny.fr
⊕ 6/I7

Théâtre National de la Colline
15 r Malte Brun, 20th
Ⓜ Gambetta
Ⓒ 01 44 62 52 00
colline.fr
⊕ Off map

Théâtre de l'Odéon
pl de l'Odéon, 6th
Ⓜ Odéon
Ⓒ 01 44 85 40 00
theatre-odeon.fr
⊕ 11/N13

Théâtre Ouvert
Jardin d'Hiver, 4bis Cité Véron, 18th
Ⓜ Blanche
Ⓒ 01 42 55 74 40
theatre-ouvert.net
⊕ 2/M2

Théâtre de la Porte Saint-Martin
18 bd St Martin, 10th
Ⓜ République
Ⓒ 01 42 08 00 32
portestmartin.com
⊕ 7/S7

Théâtre du Soleil
route du Champ de Manoeuvre, 12th
Ⓜ Château de Vincennes + shuttle bus
Ⓒ 01 43 74 24 08
theatre-du-soleil.fr
⊕ Off map

Théâtre de la Tempête
route du Champ de Manoeuvre, 12th
Ⓜ Château de Vincennes + shuttle bus
Ⓒ 01 43 28 36 36
la-tempete.fr
⊕ Off map

06

See page 9 to scan the directory

07

DESIGNER HOTELS
AND CREATIVE ROOMS

Hôtel Jardin de l'Odéon, 6th

Hôtel du Petit Moulin
29-31 rue du Poitou, 3rd

Hotels are part of the myth of avant-garde Paris, the Montparnasse of artists, the Saint-Germain-des-Prés of writers and jazz, serving as lodgings – and meeting points – for those who have always flocked to the city from all over the world.

Artists in the bedroom

Several recent hotels have become outlets for artistic creativity. **Hôtel le A** – for Art – is a collaboration between decorator Frédéric Méchiche and artist Fabrice Hyber. There are paintings by Hyber in the bedrooms and the lounge and a huge ceramic tile panel over the atrium, plus a well stocked library of art books.

07

In up-and-coming Pigalle, the trendy **Hôtel Amour** is the deliberately low-tech, non-design brainchild of graffiti artist-cum-nightclub entrepreneur André and a scion of the Costes family, Thierry. Contemporary art is cleverly mixed with retro furniture, lighting found at flea markets and loud Marikmekko print curtains. Some rooms have been conceived by artists, including Sophie Calle, illustrator Pierre le Tan, graphic design duo M/M (Paris) and André himself.

Nearby, on exclusive avenue Junot, the **Hôtel Particulier de Montmartre** is an arty five-suite hideaway, where modern design classics, baroque antiques and a tangled garden meet rooms decorated by artists including Martine Aballéa, Philippe Mayaux and Natacha Lesueur. Meanwhile, the revamped **Hôtel des Académies et des Arts** displays works by grafitti artist Jérôme Mesnager and sculptor Sophie de Watrigant, and artists's videos are projected in its movie salon.

The **Hôtel des Grands Hommes**, where "pope of Surrealism" André Breton invented automatic writing in 1919, maintains its arty ethos as part of Les Hôtels Paris Rive Gauche. This group of six Left Bank hotels, which also includes the **Hôtel de la Sorbonne** and the **Hôtel-Résidence Henri IV**, encourages artistic creation by inviting up-and-coming photographers to spend a night in one of the hotels and then create one photographic work plus an accompanying text visible on the website www.hotels-paris-rive-gauche.com, along with a portfolio of the photographer's work.

Designer hotels

Other hotels have become showcases for French design talents or changing exhibitions. From the same team as the slick **Murano Urban Resort**, **Kube Hotel**, located in a gritty area north of Gare du Nord, combines witty high-tech design, sexy underlit beds, fake fur curtains and open-plan bathrooms, as well as the Ice Kube bar designed by artist Laurent Saksik. The gleaming white **Hôtel Costes K** by Spanish architect Ricardo Bofill is a suitable showcase for a collection of contemporary art and furniture. Hiding behind a Belle Epoque facade, the **Hôtel Sezz**, designed by Christophe Pillet, is the most rigorous of Paris's new design hotels. Walls clad in dark grey stone are warmed up by thick, colourful carpets, hand-blown Murano lamps and changing contemporary art displays.

A prized insider address is Azzedine Alaïa's **Three Rooms**, three sophisticated apartments next to the fashion designer's Marais boutique. Inside you will find furniture and lighting from Alaïa's collection of modern design classics by Jean Prouvé, Jean Nouvel, Serge Mouille, Arne Jakobsen and Pierre Paulin. Meanwhile, Christian Lacroix's **Hôtel du Petit Moulin** spans two 17th century houses in the Marais and is awash with lush fabrics, daring colour combinations and eclectic lights and trompe l'oeil drawings.

07

It's refreshing to see the arrival of some affordable design hotels like the friendly **Hôtel Mayet**, the all black and white **Standard Hôtel**, with its funky lamps by Mat & Jewski, the trendy **Le Général** and the

Hôtel Mayet
3 rue Mayet, 6th

Hôtel Duo, the latter two both designed by Jean-Philippe Nuël. Also in this category is the invigorating **Five Hôtel**, where, along with glittery fibreoptics and graphic bathroom tiles, you can choose the ambient fragrances to be wafted around your room.

Arty antecedents

Between the wars, Dada and Surrealist writers and artists and the painters of the École de Paris congregated on the Left Bank. Montparnasse became an international melting pot of artists and intellectuals. Many of them stayed at the **Hôtel Istria**, including artists Francis Picabia, Marcel Duchamp, Man Ray, Fernand Léger, cabaret star Josephine Baker, composer Eric Satie and writers Louis Aragon, Vladimir Mayakovsky and Rainer Maria Rilke. The **Hôtel Villa des Artistes,** where Ernest Hemingway, Modigliani and Samuel Beckett stayed, was also popular.

07

Dali favoured **Le Meurice**; Pissarro painted from his room at the **Hôtel du Louvre,** while *nouveau réaliste* Arman often stayed at the **Hôtel Lutétia**, whose Arman suite still contains some of his works of art and African pieces from his collection. No boho artist's garret, either, for Russian emigré Boris Pastoukhoff. The successful society portrait painter stayed at the elegant **Hôtel Lancaster** in the 1930s, leaving behind paintings in lieu of payment, several of them still on the walls. Marlene Dietrich – whose suite has been preserved – also lived here for three years in the 1930s, setting a precedent for more recent film-star guests including Ewan McGregor, Jeremy Irons, David Lynch and Sir Alec Guinness.

Literary inspiration

Hotels formed part of Paris's literary myth, offering the necessary anonymity of a room of one's own. Saint-Germain-des-Prés, the traditional home of publishing houses and the birthplace of the café, provided the essential ingredients for the literary exile.

Simone de Beauvoir spent most of her life moving between assorted, usually seedy, Left Bank hotels "*sans comfort*". Among her numerous addresses were the now chic, but then wretched, **Hôtel d'Aubusson** in Saint-Germain and the **Hôtel Mistral**, near the Montparnasse cemetery, where she and Sartre – the original liberated couple – had (separate) rooms. The latter is still a lovingly-tended, family-run hotel.

L'Hôtel still has Oscar Wilde's room, albeit in more luxurious form with mahogany furniture and peacock wallpaper, than when the writer died in 1900 at what was then the scruffy Hôtel d'Alsace. "My wallpaper and I are fighting a duel to the death. One or the-other of us has to go" he wrote prophetically a few days before he died. More recently in the 1970s and 80s, Argentine writer Jorge-Luis Borges stayed here frequently. The **Relais Hôtel Vieux Paris** has also gone up in the world since this 15th-century building was discovered by Beat poets William Burroughs, Brion Gysin and Alain Ginsberg in the 1950s, then a simple hotel with one bath for 42 rooms and low monthly room rates.

The ultimate literary hotel is **Hôtel La Louisiane**, where Egyptian writer Albert Cossery, now in his 90s, has lived for over half a century. It was once a hotbed of existentialism – home to De Beauvoir, Sartre (who wrote *La Nausée* here) and singer-muse Juliette Gréco; later, jazzmen and film makers Louis Malle, Bertrand Tavernier and Quentin Tarentino stayed here. La Louisiane keeps up the artistic tradition with prices that are low for the district, circa-1980 brown floral carpet, gallery posters in the lobby and a slightly threadbare look (although bathrooms have been redone).

07

Film star chic

Staying in them or acting in them – some hotels get all the luck when it comes to starlet action. Stanley Donen's romantic jewel-heist *Charade* (1963) was first

Hôtel de Crillon
10 place de la Concorde, 8th

made starring Audrey Hepburn and Cary Grant at the **Hôtel Saint-Jacques** in the Latin Quarter, then remade in 2002 by Jonathan Demme as *The Truth About Charlie*, featuring Thandie Newton and Mark Wahlberg. For the remake, the action switched to rue Saint-Lazare and the art nouveau Hôtel des Croisés, subsequently renamed the **Hôtel Langlois** – after the name Demme gave it in the film in tribute to Cinémathèque founder Henri Langlois.

More used to the jet set is the **Grand Hôtel Inter-continental**, where Harrison Ford stays in Polanski's *Frantic* (1988), also home to Julia Roberts in Altman's fashion-world satire *Prêt-à-Porter* (1994). Opened for the 1900 Great Exhibition, complete with an iron-framed salon designed by Gustave Eiffel, the **Hôtel Concorde Saint-Lazare** is put to good use by Virginie Ledoyen, who plays a chambermaid in Benoît Jacquot's near real-time *La Fille Seule* (1995).

Grandest of the lot is the palatial **Hôtel de Crillon**, dripping with marble and crystal chandeliers, where Julia Ormond stayed in Sydney Pollack's 1995 remake of *Sabrina*. A swarm of paparazzi and fans usually hangs out in front of the magnificent palace, which has also hosted a good dose of real-life film stars, from Charlie Chaplin to Tom Hanks and Uma Thurman.

07

Price indications are for a double room: € up to €100; €€ €101–€200; €€€ €201–€350; €€€€ €351 and over.

Designer hotels

Artus Hôtel €€€
34 r de Buci, 6th
Ⓜ Mabillon
Ⓣ 01 43 29 07 20
artushotel.com
⊕ 11/N12

Hôtel Duo €€
11 r du Temple, 4th
Ⓜ Hôtel de Ville
Ⓣ 01 42 72 72 22
duoparis.com
⊕ 11/R10

Kube Rooms & Bars €€€
1-5 passage Ruelle, 18th
Ⓜ La Chapelle
Ⓣ 01 42 05 20 00
kubehotel.com
⊕ 3/S1

Five Hôtel €€
3 r Flatters, 5th
Ⓜ Gobelins
Ⓣ 01 43 31 74 21
thefivehotel.com
⊕ 15/R17

Hôtel Mayet €€
3 r Mayet, 6th
Ⓜ Duroc
Ⓣ 01 47 83 21 35
mayet.com
⊕ 14/J15

Murano Urban Resort €€€€
13 bd du Temple, 3rd
Ⓜ Filles du Calvaire
Ⓣ 01 42 71 20 00
muranoresort.com
⊕ 8/U8

Le Général €€
5-7 r Rampon, 11th
Ⓜ République
Ⓣ 01 47 00 41 57
legeneralhotel.com
⊕ 8/U8

Hôtel du Petit Moulin €€
29-31 r de Poitou, 3rd
Ⓜ St Sébastien Froissart
Ⓣ 01 42 74 10 10
hoteldupetitmoulin.com
⊕ 11-12/T10

Standard Hôtel €€
29 r des Taillandiers, 11th
Ⓜ Bastille
Ⓣ 01 48 05 30 97
standard-hotel.com.
⊕ 12/W12

Hôtel Costes K €€€€
81 av Kléber, 16th
Ⓜ Boissière
Ⓣ 01 44 05 75 75
hotelcostesk.com
⊕ 6/M8

Hôtel Sezz €€€€
6 av Frémiet, 16th
Ⓜ Passy
Ⓣ 01 56 75 26 26
hotelsezz.com
⊕ 9/B11

Three Rooms €€€€
5 r de Moussy, 4th
Ⓜ Hôtel de Ville
Ⓣ 01 44 78 92 00
⊕ 11/R11

Arty antecedents

Hôtel Istria €€
29 r Campagne
Première, 14th
Ⓜ Vavin
Ⓒ 01 43 20 91 82
istria-paris-hotel.com
✛ 14/M17

Hôtel du Louvre €€€€
pl André Malraux, 1st
Ⓜ Palais Royal
Ⓒ 01 44 58 38 38
hoteldulouvre.com
✛ 6/M9

Hôtel Villa des Artistes €€
9 r de la Grande
Chaumière, 6th
Ⓜ Vavin
Ⓒ 01 43 26 60 86
villa-artistes.com
✛ 6/L7

Hôtel Lancaster €€€€
7 r de Berri, 8th
Ⓜ George V
Ⓒ 01 40 76 40 76
hotel-lancaster.fr
✛ 5/F6

Hôtel Lutétia €€€€
45 bd Raspail, 6th
Ⓜ Sèvres Babylone
Ⓒ 01 49 54 46 46
lutetia-paris.com
✛ 10/K13

Le Meurice €€€€
228 r de Rivoli, 1st
Ⓜ Tuileries
Ⓒ 01 44 58 10 10
meuricehotel.com
✛ 6/M9

Literary inspiration

L'Hôtel €€€
13 r des Beaux Arts, 6th
Ⓜ Mabillon
Ⓒ 01 44 41 99 00
l-hotel.com
✛ 11/N12

Hôtel La Louisiane €
60 r de Seine, 6th
Ⓜ Mabillon
Ⓒ 01 44 32 17 17
hotel-lalouisiane.com
✛ 11/N12

Hôtel du Pont Royal €€€€
7 r de Montalembert, 7th
Ⓜ Rue de Bac
hotel-pont-royal.com
✛ 10/L11

07

Hôtel d'Aubusson €€€
33 r Dauphine, 6th
Ⓜ Odéon
Ⓒ 01 43 29 43 43
hoteldaubusson.com
✛ 11/N12

Hôtel Mistral €
24 r Cels, 14th
Ⓜ Gaîté
Ⓒ 01 43 20 25 4
hotel-mistral-paris.com
✛ 14/K17

**Relais Hôtel Vieux
Paris** €€€
9 r Gît le Coeur, 6th
Ⓜ Odéon
Ⓒ 01 44 32 15 90
paris-hotel-vieuxparis.com
✛ 11/O12

Film star chic

Grand Hôtel Intercontinental €€€€
2 r Scribe, 9th
Ⓜ Opéra
Ⓒ 01 40 07 32 32
paris-le-grand.
intercontinental.com
✥ 6/L6

Hôtel Concorde St-Lazare €€€
108 r St-Lazare, 8th
Ⓜ St Lazare
Ⓒ 01 40 08 44 44
concordestlazare-paris.com
✥ 2-6/L5

Hôtel Costes €€€€
239 r St-Honoré, 1st
Ⓜ Tuileries
Ⓒ 01 42 44 50 00
hotelcostes.com
✥ 6/M8

Hôtel de Crillon €€€€
10 pl de la Concorde, 8th
Ⓜ Concorde
Ⓒ 01 44 71 15 00
crillon.com
✥ 6/J8

Hôtel Langlois €€
63 r St-Lazare, 9th
Ⓜ Trinité
Ⓒ 01 48 74 78 24
hotel-langlois.com
✥ 2-6/L5

Hôtel St-Jacques €
35 r des Ecoles, 5th
Ⓜ Maubert Mutualité
Ⓒ 01 44 07 45 45
hotel-saintjacques.com
✥ 15/Q15

Hôtel Lutétia
45 boulevard Raspail, 6th

Artists in the bedroom

Hôtel le A' €€€
4 r d'Artois, 8th
Ⓜ Franklin D Roosevelt
Ⓣ 01 42 56 99 99
paris-hotel-a.com
⊕ 5-6/G6

**Hôtel des Grands
Hommes** €€
17 pl du Panthéon, 5th
®⃝ Luxembourg
Ⓣ 01 46 34 19 60
hoteldesgrandshommes.
com
⊕ 15/P15

**Hôtel Particulier de
Montmartre** €€€
23 av Junot, 17th
Ⓜ Lamarck Caulaincourt
hotel-particulier-
montmartre.com
⊕ Off map

**Hôtel des Académies
et des Arts** €€€
15 r de la Grande
Chaumière, 6th
Ⓜ Vavin
Ⓣ 01 43 26 66 44
hoteldesacademies.fr
⊕ 14/I17

**Hôtel Jardin de
l'Odéon** €€
7 r Casimir
Delavigne, 6th
Ⓜ Odéon
Ⓣ 01 53 10 28 50
⊕ 11-15/N14

**Hôtel Résidence
Henri IV** €€
50 r des Bernardins, 5th
Ⓜ Cardinal Lemoine
Ⓣ 01 44 41 31 81
residencehenry4.com
⊕ 11-15/Q14

Hôtel Amour €€
8 r de Navarin, 9th
Ⓜ St Georges
Ⓣ 01 48 78 31 80
hotelamour.com
⊕ 3/N3

Hôtel du Panthéon €€
19 pl du Panthéon, 5th
®⃝ Luxembourg
Ⓣ 01 43 54 32 95
hoteldupantheon.com
⊕ 15/P15

Hôtel de la Sorbonne €
6 r Victor Cousin, 5th
®⃝ Luxembourg
Ⓣ 01 43 54 58 08
hotelsorbonne.com
⊕ 15/O15

07

See page 9
to scan the
directory

08

RESTAURANTS
AND CAFES

Chez Nenesse
17 rue de Saintonge, 3rd

Previous page: Georges
Centre Pompidou,
rue Rambuteau, 4th

Paris restaurants and cafés exist to suit all artistic tastes, from literary classics to new conceptual restaurants, places to eat while listening to mellow jazz, bars for intense debate and fashionable brasseries where you might just rub shoulders with writers and film stars.

Museum eats

Every museum worth its salt now has to have its own trendy restaurant. **Transversal**, in the MAC/VAL, has taken the artistic project to heart: by day, you can choose from and combine numbered raw ingredients conceived like artists's materials, or order updated bistro fare; by night, there are experimental tasting plates. Likewise, **Le Saut du Loup** at the Musée des Arts Décoratifs has appropriate design cred in the form of a black-and-white interior by Philippe Boisselier, chairs by Jean-Philippe Nuël and Charles Eames, stools by Konstantin Grcic, all combined with artily deconstructed dishes by chef Pascal Bernier.

At **Tokyo Eat**, an open kitchen, spaceship-like lamps and lots of fashionable carpaccios and world flavours suit the voluminous, distressed-chic Palais de Tokyo.

08

At **Georges**, at the top of the Centre Pompidou, it's the view and the arty design with globular metallic pods by architects Jacob and MacFarlane that count, rather than the modish Costes brothers brasserie fare. Jean Nouvel-designed **Les Ombres**, at the Musée du Quai Branly, also has great views, but young chef Arno Busquet has been winning acclaim, too, adding global spices to Gallic ingredients.

Art on a plate

Eating out is a crucial element of French culture, and cooking itself is often considered an art form. Amid the battle of the ancients and the moderns, **Pierre Gagnaire** is considered by some as the most experimental chef working in Paris today. He often collaborates with scientist Hervé This to get the most taste, and colour, at the right price, in his jewel-like inventions.

Another top chef challenging culinary boundaries is veteran Alain Senderens, who, helped by designer Noé Duchaufour-Lawrence, has metamorphised Art Nouveau Lucas Carton into space-age **Senderens**. Gilles Choukroun, one of the leaders of young chefs movement Générations.C, has a showcase for his daring combinations such as beetroot, liquorice, grapefruit and tuna at **Angl' Opéra**. At **Ze Kitchen Galerie**, William Ledeuil combines Asian-influenced fusion cooking with a love of painting, using ingredients as if constructing a canvas, and exhibiting artists such as Tony Soulié, Jacques Bosser and Daniel Humair in the restaurant.

One of Paris's most talked about young chefs is Inaki Aizpitarte, whose instinctive cooking at **Le Chateaubriand** has made him an instant hit. Keeping up the modern bistro trend, haute-cuisine-trained Philippe Delacourcelle's inventive dishes at **Le Pré Verre** might involve spices, wood-smoked potato puree, quinoa or parsley ice cream – and bargain prices.

Gallery rendez-vous

Gallery owners like to lunch at **Chez Nenesse**, the very picture of a provincial bistro hiding amid Marais sophistication, or pile into the crowded dining room at wine bistro **Le Baromètre. Café Beaubourg** is a must for art world gossip thanks to its ringside view of the Centre Pompidou. A long-standing favourite for its couscous royale and the warm welcome is **Chez Omar**, while the **Andy Wahloo** bar (sidekick of Le 404), with its Moroccan snacks, paint-can stools and late-night DJs has an arty post-vernissage vibe. In Saint-Germain, **Bistrot Mazarin** and **La Palette** are institutions for art students and gallerists alike. Champs-Elysées gallery-goers relax amid Ingo Maurer furniture in the café at the **Artcurial** auction house and gallery.

08

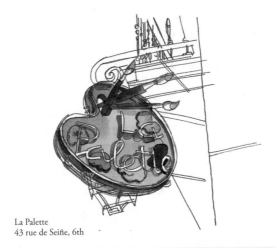

La Palette
43 rue de Seine, 6th

Vegetating art

Exploring the relationship between contemporary art and food, as well as promoting healthy eating, exhibitions at the fruit and vegetable board's **Galerie Fraich'Attitude** are diverse. It might be displays by artists like Dorothée Selz combined with work by culinary performers Mimi Oka and Doug Fitch or it might be an initiative by designer Séphane Bureaux to develop new tools for chefs.

Galerie Fraich'Attitude,
60 rue du Fbg-Poissonnière 10th
Tel: 01 49 49 15 15
galeriefraichattitude.fr

Designed by artists

Sometimes it's the restaurants themselves that are the artworks. **Restaurant Etienne Marcel**, part of the Costes brothers's empire, is a collaboration between artists Pierre Huyghe, Philippe Pareno and graphic design duo M/M (Paris). Jérôme Foucaud and Laurent Saksik conceived the **Ice Kube** at Kube Rooms & Bars, with ice walls animated by constantly changing coloured LEDs. Inside, kept at a steady -5°C, bar, tables and even vodka glasses are also all made from ice. The buzzing bistro at the **Hôtel Amour**, created by the artist André, has a drop-dead chic retro decor of flea market lights and formica.

Arty Montparnasse

Though more likely to be frequented by cinema-goers today, Montparnasse's cafés and brasseries were an essential part of the creative buzz that once filled this area. **La Coupole**, which opened in 1927 as a *bar américain* with columns painted by different artists, continues to be a favourite with Parisians as well as tourists, for superb shellfish and people-watching. **La Closerie des Lilas**, now elegant rather than boho, still gets its share of actors and writers, and you can enjoy sitting at a table once frequented by Apollinaire, Picasso, Man Ray or Trotsky. **Le Dôme**, Simone de Beauvoir's favourite café, has become a grandiose fish

08

La Closerie des Lilas
171 boulevard du Montparnasse, 6th

restaurant. Artists still occasionally drop in from the studios next door at convivial bistro **Wadja**, while **Le Caméléon** has made a comeback with new ownership and updated bistro cuisine.

Saint-Germain's literary past is still best captured by its famous cafés. The **Café de Flore**, Dada and Surrealist hangout and birthplace of Existentialism, is still favoured by *germanopratines* like Frederic Beigbeder, Bernard-Henri Lévy and Eric Rohmer, and hosts geopolitical debates and English philosophy sessions upstairs. Its eternal rival **Les Deux Magots** draws tourists on the terrace and editors inside, and like the Flore, awards a literary prize.

Le Voltaire, the quietly chic riverside brasserie once frequented by Max Ernst, is still a discreet haunt of celebrities, from Jean-Paul Belmondo to Italian model-turned-singer Carla Bruni. Budget bistro **Polidor** has been packing in impoverished writers and students ever since Verlaine, while the **Bar du Lutétia** remains an elegant haunt of publishers, writers and film stars. Over on the Right Bank is **Drouant**, now run by Alsace chef Antoine Westermann, where the ten members of the Académie Goncourt meet each year to choose the laureat of France's most prestigious fiction prize.

08

Les Deux Magots
6 place Saint Germain, 6th

New literary cafés

A new species of literary café offers food and well-stocked bookshelves to suit all tastes. In the Marais, **La Belle Hortense**, half-bookshop, half-wine bar, puts on readings, debates, wine tastings and photo exhibitions, while the sophisticated **Le Fumoir** combines an elegant cocktail bar and restaurant, with a library where you can exchange your books or settle down to read on comfortable chesterfield sofas. Brasserie and lounge bar **Les Editeurs** plays on Saint-Germain's literary roots, with a literary prize and a substantial library to browse through. Although most visitors prefer the terrace of the **Café de la Mairie**, literary aficionados skulk upstairs for literary readings and debates each Monday. Convivial literary café and restaurant **Ogre à Plumes** has books to read in situ, holds readings and stages meetings of the British Society of Authors.

Film hangouts

08

At the Cinéma des Cinéastes, wine bar **Le Père Lathuille** – named after a bar painted by Manet – is a gathering place for film-makers and wine lovers, with a cinematic nod in its menu headings. A fashionable rendez-vous for film producers and actors is **Fouquet's** on the Champs-Elysées, which hosts the annual dinner for the César film awards; the names of winning films are engraved in the pavement outside.

La Belle Hortense
31 rue Vieille du Temple, 4th

Other places have gained cult status on screen: train station brasserie **Le Train Bleu** features in Luc Besson's *Nikita* (1990) and is also the setting for Rowan Atkinson's discovery of oysters in *Mr Bean's Holiday* (2007). The **Pause Café**, a favourite with starlets and the best terrace in the Bastille, features in Klapisch's *Chacun cherche son chat* (1995).

Before or after a show

After an evening at the Théâtre des Champs-Elysées, **La Maison Blanche**, situated up on the roof, offers a spectacular eyrie with its suave white interior, view of the Eiffel Tower and mod Med cooking devised by the Pourcel twins. The defiantly non-design **Bar des Théâtres** is a rare real café in this area. **Brasserie Bofinger** is a favourite for oysters after the Opéra Bastille, and the luxurious **Café de la Paix** prolongs the glamour of the Palais Garnier. At the Théâtre Edouard VII, the **Café Guitry** is run by Andrée Zana Murat, wife of the theatre's actor-director Bernard Murat, and the modern French cooking is making it a destination in its own right.

08

Jazz with dinner

Le Bilboquet, last of the Saint-Germain jazz clubs, welcomed Miles Davis and Charlie Parker in its heyday but is now firmly in the easy listening register of blues

Viaduc Café
43 avenue Daumesnil, 12th

and swing. There's more interesting programming at **Le Petit Journal Montparnasse**, where regulars include pianist Jacky Terrasson and veteran Cameroon-born saxophonist Manu Dibango. At its smaller sibling, **Le Petit Journal St-Michel**, the mood is strictly New Orleans dixieland. Dine on deck on the **La Balle au Bond** houseboat and then go down below for live jazz or *chanson*; or have a cocktail at the gorgeous **China Club** before live jazz, soul or funk in the cellar from Thursday to Saturday nights. Sunday jazz brunch is a fixture at **Le Viaduc Café**, set in a dramatic railway arch of the Viaduc des Arts.

Creative cafés & music bars

A new generation of original arty bars has accompanied the cultural shift to northeast Paris, among them **Abracadabar** and **Café Chérie**, on either side of La Villette, with their blend of live music, DJs and art exhibitions. **Lou Pascalou**, the scene for art shows, monthly short film and slam poetry sessions, and occasional concerts, is a Ménilmontant fixture that has outlived many more recent arrivals. Artily converted train station **La Flèche d'Or** puts on free 30-minute music showcases, and monthly We Are the Lions indie nights. At **OPA**, a converted industrial space near the Bastille, astute programming of rock, *chanson* and electro has seen rising names like Jad Wio, Emilie Simon and Mlle K. pass through.

08

Museum eats

Café des Techniques
Musée des Arts et Métiers,
r Réaumur, 3rd
Ⓜ Arts et Métiers
ⓒ 01 53 01 82 83
arts-et-metiers.net
✣ 7/S8

Georges
Centre Pompidou,
r Rambuteau, 4th
Ⓜ Rambuteau
ⓒ 01 44 78 47 99
centrepompidou.fr
✣ 11/Q10

Les Ombres
Musée du Quai Branly,
27 quai Branly, 7th
Ⓜ Alma Marceau
ⓒ 01 47 53 68 00
lesombres-restaurant.com
✣ 9/E10

Le Saut du Loup
Musée des Arts Décoratifs,
107 r de Rivoli, 1st
Ⓜ Palais Royal
ⓒ 01 42 25 49 55
lesautduloup.com
✣ 6/M9

Tokyo Eat
Palais de Tokyo, 13 av du
Président Wilson, 16th
Ⓜ Alma Marceau
ⓒ 01 47 20 00 20
palaisdetokyo.com
✣ 5/E9

Transversal
MAC/VAL, carrefour de la
Libération, Vitry-sur-Seine
Ⓜ Porte de Choisy, then
bus 183
ⓒ 01 55 53 09 93
restaurant-transversal.com
✣ Off map

Art on a plate

Angl'Opéra
39 av de l'Opéra, 2nd
Ⓜ Opéra
ⓒ 01 42 61 86 25
anglopera.com
✣ 6/M7

Le Chateaubriand
129 av Parmentier, 11th
Ⓜ Goncourt
ⓒ 01 43 57 45 95
✣ 8/W9

Pierre Gagnaire
6 r Balzac, 8th
Ⓜ Charles de Gaulle Etoile
ⓒ 01 58 36 12 50
pierre-gagnaire.com
✣ 5/E6

Le Pré Verre
8 r Thénard, 5th
Ⓜ Maubert Mutualité
ⓒ 01 43 54 59 47
lepreverre.com
✣ 11-15/P14

Senderens
9 pl de la Madeleine, 8th
Ⓜ Madeleine
ⓒ 01 42 65 22 90
senderens.fr
✣ 6/K7

Ze Kitchen Galerie
4 r des Grands Augustins, 6th
Ⓜ St Michel
ⓒ 01 44 32 00 32
zekitchengalerie.fr
✣ 11/O12

Designed by artists

Hôtel Amour
8 r de Navarin, 9th
Ⓜ St Georges
ⓒ 01 48 78 31 80
hotelamour.com
✣ 3/N3

Ice Kube
Kube Rooms & Bars,
1-5 passage Ruelle, 18th
Ⓜ La Chapelle
ⓒ 01 42 05 20 00
Kubehotel.com
✣ 3/S1

Restaurant Etienne Marcel
34 r Etienne Marcel, 2nd
Ⓜ Etienne Marcel
ⓒ 01 45 08 01 03
✣ 7/P9

Gallery rendez-vous

Andy Wahloo
69 r des Gravilliers, 3rd
Ⓜ Arts et Métiers
Ⓒ 01 42 71 20 38
⊕ 7/R9

Artcurial
7 Rond Point des
Champs Elysées, 8th
Ⓜ Franklin D Roosevelt
Ⓒ 01 42 99 20 20
artcurial.com
⊕ 6/H7

Le Baromètre
17 r Charlot, 3rd
Ⓜ St Sebastien Froissart
Ⓒ 01 48 87 04 54
⊕ 7-8/T9

Bistrot Mazarin
42 r Mazarine, 6th
Ⓜ Mabillon
Ⓒ 01 43 29 99 01
bistrotmazarin.com
⊕ 11/N12

Café Beaubourg
43 r St Merri, 4th
Ⓜ Hôtel de Ville
Ⓒ 01 48 87 63 96
⊕ 11/R10

Café des Musées
49 r de Turenne, 3rd
Ⓜ Chemin Vert
Ⓒ 01 42 72 96 17
⊕ 11-12/T11

Chez Nenesse
17 r de Saintonge, 3rd
Ⓜ Filles du Calvaire
Ⓒ 01 42 78 46 49
⊕ 7-8/T9

Chez Omar
47 r de Bretagne, 3rd
Ⓜ Arts et Métiers
Ⓒ 01 42 72 36 26
⊕ 7-8/T9

La Palette
43 r de Seine, 6th
Ⓜ St Germain des Prés
Ⓒ 01 43 26 68 15
⊕ 11/N12

Arty Montparnasse

Le Caméléon
6 r de Chevreuse, 6th
Ⓜ Vavin
Ⓒ 01 43 27 43 27
⊕ 14/M17

La Closerie des Lilas
171 bd du
Montparnasse, 6th
Ⓡ Port Royal
Ⓒ 01 40 51 34 50
⊕ 14/M17

La Coupole
102 bd du
Montparnasse, 14th
Ⓜ Vavin
Ⓒ 01 43 20 14 20
flobrasseries.com/
coupoleparis/
⊕ 14/L16

Le Dôme
108 bd du
Montparnasse, 14th
Ⓜ Vavin
Ⓒ 01 43 35 25 81
⊕ 14/L16

La Rotonde
105 bd du Montparnasse,
6th
Ⓜ Vavin
Ⓒ 01 43 26 48 26
rotondemontparnasse.com
⊕ 14/L16

Wadja
10 r de la Grande
Chaumière, 6th
Ⓜ Vavin
Ⓒ 01 46 33 02 02
⊕ 14/L17

08

Creative cafés & music bars

Abracadabar
123 av Jean Jaurès, 19th
Ⓜ Laumière
Ⓒ 01 42 03 18 04
abracadabar.fr
⊕ 4/Y1

L'Ile Enchantée
65 bd de la Villette, 19th
Ⓜ Belleville
Ⓒ 01 42 01 67 99
⊕ 4-8/W5

Lou Pascalou
14 r des Panoyaux, 20th
Ⓜ Ménilmontant
Ⓒ 01 46 36 78 10
loupascalou.com
⊕ 8/Z8

Café Chérie
44 bd de la Villette, 19th
Ⓜ Belleville
Ⓒ 01 42 02 02 05
cafecherie.blogspot.com
⊕ 4-8/W5

Le Limonaire
18 cité Bergère, 9th
Ⓜ Grands Boulevards
Ⓒ 01 45 23 33 33
limonaire.free.fr
⊕ 7/P6

OPA
9 r Biscornet, 12th
Ⓜ Bastille
Ⓒ 01 46 28 12 90
opa.paris.free.fr
⊕ 12-16/V14

La Flèche d'Or
102bis r de Bagnolet, 20th
Ⓜ Gambetta
Ⓒ 01 44 64 01 02
flechedor.fr
⊕ Off map

Living B'art
15 r La Vieuville, 18th
Ⓜ Abbesses
Ⓒ 01 42 52 85 34
livingbart.free.fr
⊕ 3/O2

Satellit Café
44 r de la Folie
Méricourt, 11th
Ⓜ Oberkampf
Ⓒ 01 47 00 48 87
satellit-café.com
⊕ 8/V9

Glitterati classics

Bar du Lutétia
Hôtel Lutétia,
45 bd Raspail, 6th
Ⓜ Sèvres Babyone
Ⓒ 01 49 54 46 46
lutetia-paris.com
⊕ 10/K13

Brasserie Wepler
18 pl de Clichy, 18th
Ⓜ Place de Clichy
Ⓒ 01 45 22 53 24
wepler.com
⊕ 2/L2

Les Deux Magots
6 pl St-Germain, 6th
Ⓜ St Germain des Prés
Ⓒ 01 45 48 55 25
lesdeuxmagots.com
⊕ 10/M12

Brasserie Lipp
151 bd St-Germain, 6th
Ⓜ St Germain des Prés
Ⓒ 01 45 48 53 91
brasserie-lipp.fr
⊕ 10/L12

Café de Flore
172 bd St-Germain, 6th
Ⓜ St Germain des Prés
Ⓒ 01 45 48 55 26
cafe-de-flore.com
⊕ 10/L12

Drouant
16-18 pl Gaillon, 2nd
Ⓜ Pyramides
drouant.com
⊕ 6/M7

**Hemingway Bar
at Le Ritz**
15 pl Vendôme, 1st
Ⓜ Madeleine
Ⓒ 01 43 16 30 31
ritzparis.com
✛ 6/L8

Polidor
41 r Monsieur le Prince, 6th
Ⓜ Odéon
Ⓒ 01 43 26 95 34
restaurantpolidor.info
ritzparis.com
✛ 11-15/O14

Le Voltaire
27 quai Voltaire, 7th
Ⓜ Rue du Bac
Ⓒ 01 42 61 17 49
✛ 10/M11

New literary cafés

La Belle Hortense
31 r Vieille du Temple, 4th
Ⓜ St Paul
Ⓒ 01 48 04 74 60
cafeine.com
✛ 11/S11

Les Editeurs
4 carrefour de l'Odéon, 6th
Ⓜ Odéon
Ⓒ 01 43 26 67 76
lesediteurs.fr
✛ 11/N13

L'Ogre à Plumes
49-51 r Jean Pierre
Timbaud, 11th
Ⓜ Parmentier
Ⓒ 01 48 06 64 39
logreaplumes.com
✛ 8/W8

Café de la Mairie
8 pl St Sulpice, 6th
Ⓜ St Sulpice
Ⓒ 01 43 26 67 82
lelitteraire.com
✛ 10/M13

Le Fumoir
6 r de l'Amiral Coligny, 1st
Ⓜ Louvre-Rivoli
Ⓒ 01 42 92 00 24
lefumoir.com
✛ 11/O10

La Passerelle
3 r St Hubert, 11th
Ⓜ Rue St Maur
Ⓒ 01 43 57 04 82
alapasserelle.org
✛ 8/X9

Film hangouts

**Bar-Tabac des Deux
Moulins**
15 r Lepic, 18th
Ⓜ Blanche
Ⓒ 01 42 54 90 50
✛ 2/M2

Pause Café
41 r de Charonne, 11th
Ⓜ Ledru Rollin
Ⓒ 01 48 06 80 33
✛ 12/W13

Le Reflet
6 r Champollion, 5th
Ⓜ Cluny La Sorbonne
Ⓒ 01 43 29 97 27
✛ 11-15/O14

08

Fouquet's
99 av des Champs Elysées,
8th
Ⓜ George V
Ⓒ 01 47 23 50 00
lucienbarriere.com
✛ 5/F6

Le Père Lathuile
Cinéma des Cinéastes,
7 av de Clichy, 17th
Ⓜ Place de Clichy
Ⓒ 01 53 42 40 00
larp.fr
✛ 2/K1

Le Train Bleu
Gare de Lyon, pl Louis
Armand, 12th
Ⓜ Gare de Lyon
Ⓒ 01 43 43 09 06
✛ 16/V15

Bar du Lutétia
Hôtel Lutétia, 45 boulevard Raspail, 6th

Before or after a show

A la Cloche d'Or
3 r Mansart, 9th
Ⓜ Blanche
Ⓒ 01 48 74 48 88
alaclochedor.com
✤ 2/M2

Bar des Théâtres
6 av Montaigne, 8th
Ⓜ Alma Marceau
Ⓒ 01 47 23 34 63
✤ 5/F8

Brasserie Bofinger
5-7 r de la Bastille, 4th
Ⓜ Bastille
Ⓒ 01 42 72 87 82
bofingerparis.com
✤ 12/U12

Café Guitry
Théâtre Edouard VII,
10 pl Edouard VII, 9th
Ⓜ Madeleine
Ⓒ 01 40 07 00 77
theatreedouard7.com
✤ 6/L6

Café de la Paix
5 pl de l'Opéra, 9th
Ⓜ Opéra
Ⓒ 01 40 07 36 36
cafedelapaix.fr
✤ 6/M6

La Maison Blanche
15 av Montaigne, 8th
Ⓜ Alma Marceau
Ⓒ 01 47 23 55 99
maison-blanche.com
✤ 5/F8

Jazz with dinner

La Balle au Bond
Apr-Sept: quai Malaquais, 6th
Ⓜ St-Germain-des-Prés
Oct-Mar: facing 35 quai
des Tournelles, 5th
Ⓜ Maubert Mutualité
Ⓒ 01 40 46 85 12
laballeaubond.fr
✤ 10/M11 -11-15/R14

Le Bilboquet
13 r St-Benoît, 6th
Ⓜ St-Germain-des-Prés
Ⓒ 01 45 48 81 84
jazzclub.bilboquet.free.fr
✤ 10/M12

China Club
50 r de Charenton, 12th
Ⓜ Ledru Rollin
Ⓒ 01 43 43 82 02
chinaclub.cc
✤ 11-16/W14

**Le Petit Journal
Montparnasse**
13 r du Commandant
Mouchotte, 14th
Ⓜ Gaîté
Ⓒ 01 43 21 56 70
petitjournal-
montparnasse.com
✤ 14/J17

**Le Petit Journal
St-Michel**
71 bd St-Michel, 5th
ⓇⒺⓇ Luxembourg
Ⓒ 01 43 26 28 59
petitjournalsaintmichel.
com
✤ 15/N16

Viaduc Café
43 av Daumesnil, 12th
Ⓜ Ledru Rollin
Ⓒ 01 44 74 70 70
viaduc-cafe.fr
✤ 12-16/W14

08

See page 9
to scan the
directory

09

SEASONAL FESTIVALS
AND EVENTS

Paris Plage
Quai de l'Hôtel de Ville, 4th

Parisians seem to be able to invent arts festivals to cover almost anything, ranging from elitist intellectual affairs to popular outdoor jamborees. Keep in touch with what's on with the listings magazines *Pariscope*, *Officiel du Spectacle* (both out Wednesday) and *Figaroscope* (with Wednesday's *Figaro*) and on www.evene.fr.

Multi-disciplinary festivities

The arts season starts with a bang in mid-September, when the city returns full of enthusiasm after the summer holidays. This is *La Rentrée*, the moment when major art exhibitions are inaugurated, commercial art galleries reopen, opera and concert halls get back into action and the highbrow **Festival d'Automne** launches a citywide programme of contemporary dance, music, theatre, art and film. The season slows down from late June and dries up to a trickle from mid-July to the end of August. Although all sorts of initiatives from the popular **Paris Plage** beach along the Seine via outdoor movies to the world music and contemporary dance of **Paris Quartier d'Eté** try to make up for the August lull, the main protagonists are out of town, so this is not the time to come for serious arts programming.

09

Art and design

Autumn has traditionally been the season when art collectors come to town for **FIAC** (Foire Internationale d'Art Contemporain), which returned to the grandiose Grand Palais in 2006, with additional exhibitors in the Cour Carrée of the Louvre. Despite its name, it mixes modern and contemporary art, with roughly half French, half foreign galleries; the winner of the Prix Marcel Duchamp, who gets a solo show at the Centre Pompidou in May, is announced during the fair. **Paris Photo** in November has quickly become an important international rendez-vous, successfully showcasing historic photography, early classics and the latest art photography trends.

There is also a growing hub of art fairs in March. The year 2007 saw the inaugural **Salon du Dessin Contemporain** contemporary drawings fair, with some 20 galleries each occupying a room of a 19th century *hôtel particulier* and specially commissioned wall drawings on the staircases. Indeed, perhaps the future of salons lies in this sort of small, highly targeted show. It is followed by **Art Paris**, featuring mainly French galleries, and the **Pavillon des Arts et du Design**, held in a marquee in the Tuileries. Originally a straightforward antiques fair, this now focuses on 20th century design along with a synergy of modern art and tribal art.

Assorted independent art salons crop up around the year. The **Salon de Montrouge** in May, which selects more than 150 artists between the ages of 20 and 40, is still considered a place to discover young artists.

Established and emerging artists exhibit in some of Saint- Germain's luxury fashion shops (Louis Vuitton, Céline and the like) in the **Parcours Saint-Germain**, a happy marriage between art and fashion. Another summer rendez-vous is **Diplômés**, pick of the year's graduates at Ensb-a (Ecole Nationale Supérieure des Beaux-Arts).

For those interested in furniture and interior trends, the Salon du Meuble in January is the professional fair but its offspring, the trend-spotting **Salon Futur Intérieur**, is open to the general public. In June, **Designer's Days** takes place in design shops on both Left and Right Banks, with late-night openings as they unveil new products, often in wittily staged settings.

Paris offers two arty night-time events: the nationwide **La Nuit des Musées** in May promotes heritage with free opening and unusual guided visits, performances, readings and music in museums from sunset to 1am. **La Nuit Blanche** in October is an incentive to stay up all night for contemporary art installations and video projections in different districts of Paris.

09

Fête de la Musique,
on the 21st of June each year

Architectural heritage

The **Journées du Patrimoine** heritage weekend is an opportunity to look around normally off-limits official buildings and historic residences, such as the Ministry of Justice on Place Vendôme and the gorgeous 18th century embassies and ministries of the Faubourg Saint-Germain. There is also a private contemporary version in June, the **Journées de la Maison Contemporaine**, arranged by the magazine *Architectures à Vivre*. It is worth checking out on the website in advance and reserving ahead, as opportunities to visit these architect-designed houses and lofts get very booked up.

Music and the performing arts

In addition to major international names programmed for the **Festival d'Automne**, the **Rencontres Chorégraphiques de Seine Saint-Denis** usually delivers some challenging encounters with leading choreographers. The more offbeat **100 Dessus Dessous** is an opportunity to discover young choreographers, often incorporating music, video and performance as well as dance. Experimental crossover dance, theatre and visual arts are on view at **Festival International EXIT** at Créteil, while traditional world music and dance can be seen at the **Festival de l'Imaginaire**. The essence of the France-wide **Fête de la Musique** on midsummer's day is free music for everyone and of every imaginable kind.

09

Jazz fans turn out for **Banlieues Bleues**, a five-week wide-ranging schedule of good French and international jazz, taking in Latin, R'N'B, blues and soul. The **Festival Jazz à Saint-Germain** has a growing reputation, featuring some of the best talents on the French scene. The Parc Floral provides a relaxed outdoor setting for first-rate jazz on weekend afternoons in the **Paris Jazz Festival**. Even more bucolic is the offbeat **Festival de Jazz Django Reinhardt**, held on an island in the Seine outside Paris, in memory of the late gypsy jazz guitarist. Eclectic world and folk music can be found in park bandstands during **Paris Quartier d'Eté**, while music is a key part of **La Goutte d'Or en Fête** held in a district of Paris with large African and North African communities.

Over the years, the **Festival les Inrocks**, staged by music magazine *Les Inrockuptibles*, has proved astute at introducing the next big thing in indie rock. Female indie has its own festival **Les Femmes s'en Mêlent**, a showcase for female musicians from Swedish singer-guitarists to Kirstin Hersh. **Rock en Seine** in August mixes international headliners (such as Beck and Radiohead in 2006), new indie, and up-and-coming native talent, in a beautiful park landscaped by Le Nôtre, while **Solidays** in July is a big charity music bash for AIDS charities at the Longchamp racetrack.

Opéra en Plein Air puts on gala-style outdoor productions (in recent years *The Barber of Seville*, *La Traviata* and *The Magic Flute*) in the Jardins du Sénat and various châteaux outside Paris including Vaux-Le-Vicomte. The more light hearted **Opéra des Rues** aims to raise the profile of opera with wandering troupes performing arias in streets and squares in the 12th and 13th *arrondissements*.

Classique au Vert, by the lake in the Parc Floral, combines a relaxed mood with an admirably varied programme that ranges from the Orchestre National d'Ile de France to the Swingle Sisters. The **Festival Chopin à Paris**, in the Orangerie de Bagatelle, focuses on Chopin but also brings in other keyboard composers. It is followed there by the wind-dominated chamber music season of the **Octuor de France**. Established and young soloists, mainly pianists, perform amid the lush vegetation of the 19th century glass and iron azalea house in the **Solistes aux Serres d'Auteuil**. There's more chamber music at the venerable **Festival de Musique de l'Orangerie de Sceaux**. Music meets architectural heritage in the **Festival d'Ile de France**, where classical and world music is performed in historic châteaux, churches and abbeys, along with **Factory**, a related jazz and electronic music season at La Cigale in Paris.

09

Paris Plage
Quai de l'Hôtel de Ville, 4th

Experimental contemporary music and dance get a showcase in **Festival Agora** at the Centre Pompidou and nearby IRCAM. Radio France also promotes contemporary creation, putting on free concerts in its **Festival Présences**, 'festival of musical creation'.

Poetry readings

Spring's **Printemps des Poètes** is a lively attempt to widen the audience for poetry through an eclectic schedule of poetry readings, musical evenings and other events in bars and bookshops. In summer, the **Marché de la Poésie** on Place Saint-Sulpice is a showcase for literally hundreds of often tiny poetry publishers. It coincides with the **Festival Franco-Anglais de Poésie**. The difficult exercise of translating poetry is a key concern at this event and translation workshops between English and French are a regular feature, followed by readings of the translated poems.

Film festivals

The first **Salon du Cinéma** was a surprising hit, catering for the French appetite for cinema with debates, lessons in special effects, and the chance to meet directors, screenwriters, actors and technicians. The municipally-sponsored **Paris Cinéma** is a more conventional film festival involving film previews, retrospectives and prizes. The **Festival International de Films des**

09

Saint-Sulpice

Femmes is an important rendezvous for films both fiction and documentary, often political, by women directors from all over the world. Among unusual festivals run by the Forum des Images are the **Etrange Festival**, for devotees of the weird, underground, experimental and gory, and the groundbreaking festival of **Pocket Films** – films made on mobile phones.

In summer, the **Festival du Cinéma en Plein Air** is the oldest outdoor festival, with French and Hollywood classics projected on a giant screen in Parc de la Villette. **Cinéma au Clair du Lune** is held in assorted Paris locations, with the bonus that many films have a link to the area in which they are screened.

Art and design

Art Paris
(March-April)
Grand Palais, av
Winston Churchill, 8th
℃ 01 56 26 52 16
artparis.fr
⊕ 6/H8

Biennale des Antiquaires
(September, next 2008)
Grand Palais, av
Winston Churchill, 8th
℃ 01 44 51 74 74
biennaledesantiquaires.com
⊕ 5/H8

Designer's Days
(June)
Various venues
designersdays.com

Diplômés
(May-June)
Ensb-a, 13 quai
Malaquais, 6th
℃ 01 47 03 50 00
ensba.fr
⊕ 11/M11

FIAC
(October)
Grand Palais, av
Winston Churchill, 8th
℃ 01 41 90 47 47
fiacparis.com
⊕ 5/H8

MAC 2000
(November)
Espace Champerret, 17th
℃ 06 14 18 42 24
mac2000-art.com
⊕ 1/D1

La Nuit Blanche
(1st Saturday in October)
Various venues
paris.fr

La Nuit des Musées
(May)
Selected museums
France-wide
nuitdesmusees.culture.fr

Parcours St Germain
(May-June)
Various venues in St
Germain des Prés, 6th
parcoursaintgermain.com
⊕ 10/M12

Paris Photo
(November)
Carrousel du Louvre, 1st
℃ 01 41 90 47 70
parisphoto.fr
10/M10

Pavillion des Arts et du Design
(March)
Jardin des Tuileries, 1st
℃ 01 44 07 21 87
⊕ 6/M9

Salon du Dessin Contemporain
(March)
Venue to be announced
℃ 01 44 07 21 87
salondudessin
contemporain.com

Salon Futur Intérieur
(January)
Paris Expo, 15th
℃ 01 40 76 45 00
salon-futurinterieur.com
⊕ Off map

Salon de Montrouge
(April-May)
Théâtre de Montrouge, pl
Emile Cresp, Montrouge
℃ 01 46 12 75 70
ville-montrouge.fr
⊕ Off map

Showoff
(October)
Espace Pierre Cardin, 8th
showoffparis.com
⊕ 6/J8

09

Multi-disciplinary festivities

Festival d'Automne
(September-December)
Various venues in Paris
and suburbs
☎ 01 53 45 17 17
festival-automne.com

Paris Plage
(July-August)
Banks of the Seine, 4th,
13th
paris.fr

Paris Quartier d'Eté
(July-August)
Various venues
☎ 01 44 94 98 00
quartierdete.com

Music and the performing arts

100 Dessus Dessous
(April)
La Villette, 19th
☎ 01 40 03 75 75
100dd.fr

Les Femmes s'en Mêlent
(April-May)
Various venues
☎ 01 43 07 53 08
lfsm.net

Festival les Inrocks
(November)
Various venues
lesinrocks.com

Banlieues Bleues
(February-April)
Various venues in Seine
St Denis
☎ 01 49 22 10 10
banlieuesbleues.fr
⊕ Off map

Festival d'Automne
(September-December)
Various venues
festival-automne.com

**Festival International
EXIT** *(March)*
MAC Créteil, pl Salvador
Allende, Créteil
☎ 01 45 13 19 19
maccreteil.com
⊕ Off map

Bose Blue Note Festival
(March-April)
Various venues
bosebluenotefestival.com

Festival de l'Imaginaire
(March-April)
Maison des Cultures
du Monde, 101 bd
Raspail, 6th
☎ 01 45 44 72 30
mcm.asso.fr
⊕ 14/L15

**Festival de Jazz Django
Reinhardt**
(Last weekend June)
Samois sur Seine
☎ 01 64 24 87 17
django.samois.free.fr

Festival Jazz à St Germain *(May)*
Various venues in St Germain des Prés, 6th
☎ 01 56 24 35 50
festivaljazzsaint germainparis.co
⊕ 10/M12

Jazz à la Villette *(September)*
Various venues at La Villette, 19th
jazzalavillette.com
⊕ Off map

Rencontres Chorégraphiques de Seine St Denis *(May)*
Various venues in Seine St Denis
☎ 01 55 82 08 08
www.rencontres choregraphiques.com

Fête de la Musique *(21st June)*
France-wide
fetedelamusique.fr

Paris Jazz Festival *(June-July)*
Parc Floral, Bois de Vincennes, 12th
paris.fr
⊕ Off map

Rock en Seine *(Last weekend in August)*
Domaine National de St Cloud
rockenseine.com
⊕ Off map

La Goutte d'Or en Fête *(June)*
Square Léon and other venues in 18th
gouttedorenfete.org
⊕ 3/R1

Paris Quartier d'Eté *(July-August)*
Various venues
☎ 01 44 94 98 00
quartierdete.com

Solidays *(July)*
Hippodrome de Longchamp, Bois de Boulogne, 16th
solidays.com
⊕ Off map

Architectural heritage

09

Journées de la Maison Contemporaine *(June)*
France-wide
maisons-contemporaines. com

Journées du Patrimoine *(3rd weekend in September)*
France-wide
journeesdupatrimoine. culture.fr

Vivre les Villes *(March)*
France-wide
vivrelesvilles.fr

Classical and opera

Classique au Vert
(August-September)
Parc Floral de Paris, Bois
de Vincennes, 12th
paris.fr
⊕ Off map

Festival Agora
(June)
Centre Pompidou and
IRCAM, 4th
www.ircam.fr
⊕ 11/Q10

Festival Chopin à Paris
(June-July)
Orangerie, Parc de
Bagatelle, Bois de
Boulogne, 16th
℃ 01 45 00 22 19
frederic-chopin.com
⊕ Off map

Festival d'Ile de France
(September- October)
Various venues
℃ 01 58 1 01 01
festival-ile-de-france.com

**Festival de Musique
de l'Orangerie de Sceaux**
(July-September)
Parc de Sceaux, Sceaux
℃ 01 46 60 07 79
festivaloranfgerie.free.fr
Tel: 01 53 20 48 60
etrangefestival.com
⊕ Off map

Festival Présences
(February)
Maison de Radio France,
116 av du Président
Kennedy, 16th
℃ 01 56 40 15 16
radiofrance.fr
⊕ 9/A12

Festival de St-Denis
(June-July)
Basilique de St-Denis and
other venues
℃ 01 48 13 06 07
festival-saint-denis.fr

Octuor de France
(July-August)
Orangerie, Parc de
Bagatelle, Bois de
Boulogne, 16th
℃ 01 42 29 07 83
octuordefrance.com
⊕ Off map

Opéra en Plein Air
(June-September)
Various venues
℃ 08 92 70 79 20
operaenpleinair.com

Opéra des Rues
(September)
Various venues, 12th, 13th
℃ 01 45 83 43 42
operadesrues.com

Sing-Along Messiah
(December)
American Cathedral, av
George V, 8th
parischoralsociety.org
⊕ 5/E7

**Solistes aux Serres
d'Auteuil**
(June-August-September)
Serres d'Auteuil, 1 av
Gordon Bennett, 16th
℃ 01 46 32 02 26
ars-mobilis.com
⊕ Off map

Poetry readings

**Festival Franco-Anglais
de la Poésie**
(June)
Various venues
festrad.com

Marché de la Poésie
(June)
pl St Sulpice, 6th
℃ 01 44 32 05 95
poesie.evous.fr
⊕ 10/M13

Printemps des Poètes
(March)
France-wide
℃ 01 53 80 08 00
printempsdespoetes.com

Film festivals

**Cinéma au Clair
de Lune**
(August)
Outdoor locations Paris
℃ 01 44 76 63 00
clairdelune.
forumdesimages.net

**Festival International
de Films de Femmes**
(March)
Maison des Arts de
Créteil, pl Salvador
Allende, Créteil
℃ 01 49 80 38 98
filmsdefemmes.com
⊕ Off map

Pocket Films
(June)
Forum des Images,
Forum des Halles, 1st
℃ 01 44 76 63 00
festivalpocketfilms.fr
⊕ 11/P10

Etrange Festival
(September)
℃ 01 53 20 48 60
etrangefestival.com

Paris Cinema
(July)
Cinemas across Paris
℃ 01 55 25 55 25
pariscinema.org

Salon du Cinéma
(January)
Paris Expo,15th
℃ 01 41 09 98 98
salonducinema.com
⊕ Off map

**Festival du Cinéma
en Plein Air**
(July-August)
Parc de la Villette, 19th
villette.com
⊕ Off map

09

See page 9
to scan the
directory

VENI, VIDI, VICI

Ecole Nationale Supérieure des Beaux-Arts
14 rue Bonaparte, 6th

Previous page: Couvent des Recollets
150 rue du Faubourg-Saint-Martin, 10th

There are plenty of ways to tap into Paris's cultural riches and develop your passion for art, film, theatre, design or art history, from high powered projects and residencies for professional artists, dancers, musicians and singers to short courses for all levels and all ages.

Art and design courses

Ecole Nationale Supérieure des Beaux-Arts, or Ensb-a, is Paris's main fine art school with artists such as Jean-Michel Alberola and Patrick Tosani as teachers. There's a five-year degree course and a post-masters programme. **Parsons School of Art,** linked to the New York design college, runs courses in fine art, design, fashion and photography in English. Both also run adult evening classes. If you're just around for a short time or simply want to spend an afternoon sketching, then stop at the old-fashioned **Académie de la Grande Chaumière**, which has barely changed in over a century. Traditional drawing, painting, sketching and life-drawing classes take place daily. No qualifications are necessary and it's possible to come for only a day – just bring materials. If your urge to create is really spur-of-the-moment pop into art supplies store Sennelier across the road.

10

Despite very different styles, **ENSCI 'Les Ateliers'** (Ecole Nationale Supérieure de Création Industrielle) and **ENSAD** (Ecole Nationale Supérieure des Arts Décoratifs) have between them produced many of the rising generation of designers, including Patrick Jouin, Matali Crasset and Christophe Pillet. ENSCI, located in an old furniture factory near Bastille, favours a multi-disciplinary approach and has a highly international intake, while ENSAD, based near the Panthéon, has a more traditional craft emphasis on furniture and interior design. **Ecole Camondo** is a school of architecture and design linked to the Musée des Arts Décoratifs. All have interesting designers among their staff.

Art history and the art market

The richness of Paris's museums makes the city a natural place to study art history. The prestigious **Ecole du Louvre** is the training ground for French museum curators, offering a three-year undergraduate course and a postgraduate course; many people also choose just to attend as an auditor, sitting in on classes with no exam or diploma at the end.

Courses at the Paris branch of **Christie's Education** naturally focus on French fine and decorative arts. The one-year diploma, taught in French, is aimed at those intending to make a career in the art market, but there

are also shorter non-diploma courses, evening classes and a course in English. **IESA** (Institut d'Etudes
Supérieures des Arts) and **EAC** run undergraduate and
postgraduate courses on art and the art market.

As the centre of the largest film industry in Europe,
Paris offers a clutch of film schools, where you can learn
all the skills necessary for directing and producing as well
as the technical aspects of film making. By far the most
prestigious is **Fémis** (alias the Ecole National Supérieure
des Métiers de l'Image et du Son), housed in the former
Pathé Studios. The tough entrance exam is open to college
graduates under 30, and courses cover film analysis and
history, with specialist sections in directing and sound.

Ecole Nationale Supérieure Louis Lumière doesn't
have the elite reputation of Fémis and is more geared
towards film industry technicians but has nonetheless
trained many French directors. Private school **EICAR**,
located amid the burgeoning film, TV production and
multimedia hub in Saint-Denis, has BA courses in
film directing and sound directing, including an international section taught in English. Also in English,
the Film Studies course at the **American University of
Paris** concentrates on film theory and criticism but also
includes workshops in film directing and editing.

10

Ecole Camondo
266 boulevard Raspail, 14th

Performing arts

Opéra National de Paris's **Atelier Lyrique** was founded by new director Gérard Mortier in 2005 with the ambition of discovering the opera stars of tomorrow, who get to perform in special opera productions and concerts at the Bastille and elsewhere. A dozen students at a time are accepted for the two-year course, following an audition before a jury presided over by Mortier.

American choreographer Carolyn Carlson's **Atelier de Paris**, based at La Cartoucherie, runs intensive three- or four-day masterclasses for professional dancers, taught by Carlson herself or visiting and associated choreographers. The Atelier de Paris also provides rehearsal facilities and production support. The **Centre National de la Danse** in the eastern suburb of Pantin is a useful resource centre for professional dancers; it also provides rehearsal space for companies, and runs a huge variety of professional training courses.

Studying theatre in Paris may not seem an obvious option for English speakers, yet Paris has three well respected international theatre schools. **Acting International**, directed by actor and film-maker Robert Cordier, a veteran of Broadway and the Actor's Studio, practices a span of European and US acting techniques. Candidates are encouraged to begin with a week- or month-long

10

introductory course, taught bilingually. Also offered is Acting American™, a course entirely in English, as well as classes on acting in front of the camera.

Ecole Jacques Lecoq is based on a theory of the dynamics of movement. It sounds flaky but its alumni have gone on to found some renowned companies, often with an experimental/populist bent, including Ariane Mnouchkine's Théâtre du Soleil, Footsbarn Theatre Company and Simon McBurney's Theatre de Complicité in the UK. Fashionable **Cours Florent** has spawned countless French screen stars, including Isabelle Adjani, Audrey Tautou, Daniel Auteuil and Guillaume Canet, with a method based on theatrical games and improvisation; there are courses for acting in English and dancing for musicals.

Studios and residencies

Numerous residency schemes exist for established artists, writers, musicians, choreographers, curators and researchers. Anyone who is still a student should check out the EU's Erasmus scheme as well as specific reciprocal exchange agreements between universities.

Residencies lasting anything from a few weeks to a few years are a vital part of **Les Mains d'Oeuvres**, encouraging collaborations between artists, dancers, musicians and film-makers. Other studios are available at the smaller **Point Ephémère**, while the **Kadist Art Foundation** offers one four- to six-month residency to international curators and artists leading up to an exhibition. **Le Pavillon**, directed by artist Ange Leccia, lives up to the Palais de Tokyo's 'laboratory' ethos. Each year around ten artists and art critics working in all media are selected from hundreds of applicants for an eight-month residency, which involves participating in some of the shows or events at the Palais de Tokyo.

The **Centre International d'Accueil et d'Echanges de Récollets** has 81 furnished, serviced flats and studios for European artists, scientists and intellectuals. To qualify you have to be sponsored by a university, research body or cultural event either in Paris or at home. An older scheme exists at the **Cité Internationale des Arts**, a 1960s complex for foreign artists and musicians. Rents are reasonable and facilities include print studios, rehearsal rooms and a small concert hall.

Another source of accommodation for foreign students and researchers, including some family flats, is the campus-like **Cité Internationale Universitaire de Paris**, whose halls of residence are spread over a lovely park. Further residential studio complexes, such as Montmartre aux Artistes, and studios located amid

10

Atelier, Buttes de Chaumont, 19th

public housing are administered by the **Direction des Affaires Culturelles de la Ville de Paris**; it is usually necessary to be affiliated to the Maison des Artistes, the French social security system for artists.

Additional opportunities will arrive in 2008, with the opening of **104**, **Cent Quatre** in northeast Paris. This colossal, municipally funded project based at the former Pompes Funèbres (municipal undertaker) will contain art, dance, theatre and film studios and intends to encourage contact between residents and local inhabitants through exhibitions and performances.

Resources and supplies

As well as the Centre Pompidou's vast public reference library, the **BPI**, curators, art historians and researchers can apply to use the **Bibliothèque Kandinsky**, the specialist library and documentation centre of the Musée National d'Art Moderne. At the same address as the Cinémathèque, the **BiFi** film library includes periodicals, video library, and photo library. Theatre professionals and academics can apply to use the library at the **SACD** (Société d'Auteurs et Compositeurs Dramatiques), which focuses on the performing arts, notably playscripts. Good art material shops include **Dubois** and old-fashioned colourist **Sennelier**.

10

Art and design courses

**Académie de la Grande
Chaumière**
14 r de la Grande
Chaumière, 6th
Ⓜ Vavin
Ⓒ 01 43 26 13 72
grande-chaumiere.fr
⊕ 14/L17

Ecole Camondo
266 bd Raspail, 14th
Ⓜ Raspail
Ⓒ 01 43 35 44 28
lesartsdecoratif.fr
⊕ 14/L17

**Ecole Nationale Supé-
rieure des Beaux-Arts**
14 r Bonaparte, 6th
Ⓜ St Germain des Prés
Ⓒ 01 47 03 50 00
ensba.fr
⊕ 10/M12

ENSAD
31 r d'Ulm, 5th
ⓇⒺⓇ Luxembourg
Ⓒ 01 42 34 97 00
ensad.fr
⊕ 15/P16

ENSCI 'Les Ateliers'
48 r St Sabin, 11th
Ⓜ Bréguet Sabin
Ⓒ 01 49 23 12 22
ensci.com
⊕ 12/V12

Istituto Marangoni
6-8 av Raymond Poincaré, 16th
Ⓜ Victor Hugo
Ⓒ 01 47 20 08 44
istitutomarangoni.com
⊕ 5/B8

**L'Institut Supérieur des
Arts Appliquées**
13 r Vauquelin, 5th
Ⓜ Censier Daubenton
Ⓒ 01 47 07 17 07
lisaa.com
⊕ 15/P17

Paris American Academy
277 r St-Jacques, 5th
ⓇⒺⓇ Luxembourg
Ⓒ 01 44 41 99 20
parisamericanacademy.edu
⊕ 11-15/P14

Parsons School of Art
14 r Letellier, 15th
Ⓜ Emile Zola
Ⓒ 01 45 77 39 66
parsons-paris.com
⊕ 13/D14

Art history and the art market

Christie's Education
4 av Bertie Albrecht, 8th
Ⓜ Ternes
Ⓒ 01 42 25 10 90
christies.com/education
⊕ 1-5/E5

**Le Club de l'Art/
Jeudis de Drouot**
19 r de la Paix, 2nd
Ⓜ Opéra
Ⓒ 01 42 46 46 48
leclubart.com
⊕ 6/M7

Drouot Formation
9 r Drouot, 9th
Ⓜ Richelieu Drouot
Ⓒ 01 48 00 20 52
gazette-drouot.com
⊕ 3-7/O5

EAC
13 r de la Grange
Batalière, 9th
Ⓜ Richelieu Drouot
Ⓒ 01 47 70 23 83
groupeeac.com
⊕ 7/O6

Ecole du Louvre
Palais du Louvre, 1st
Ⓜ Palais Royal
Ⓒ 01 55 35 18 00
ecoledulouvre.fr
⊕ 11/N10

IESA
5 av de l'Opéra, 1st
Ⓜ Palais Royal
Ⓒ 01 42 86 57 01
iesa.info
⊕ 6/M7

Film schools

American University of Paris
31 av Bosquet, 7th
Ⓜ La Tour Maubourg
Ⓣ 01 40 62 06 00
aup.fr
⊕ 9/F11

Conservatoire Libre du Cinéma Français
9 quai de Oise, 19th
Ⓜ Crimée
Ⓣ 01 40 36 19 19
clcf.com
⊕ Off map

Ecole Nat. Supérieure Louis Lumière
7 allée du Promontoire, 93161 Noisy le Grand
Ⓣ 01 48 15 40 10
ens-louis-lumiere.fr
⊕ Off map

Ecole Sup. Libre d'Etudes Cinématographiques
21 r de Cîteaux, 12th
Ⓜ Reuilly Diderot
Ⓣ 01 43 42 43 22
esec.edu
⊕ 12-16/X14

EICAR
50 av du Président Wilson, 93214 La Plaine St Denis
Ⓜ Porte de la Chapelle
Ⓣ 01 49 98 11 11
eicar.fr
⊕ Off map

Fémis
6 r Francoeur, 18th
Ⓜ Jules Joffrin
Ⓣ 01 53 41 21 00
femis.fr
⊕ Off map

Performing arts

Acting International
55 r des Alouettes, 19th
Ⓜ Botzaris
Ⓣ 01 42 00 06 79
acting-international.com
⊕ 4/Ÿ4

Atelier Lyrique
Opéra de Paris,
120 r de Lyon, 12th
Ⓜ Bastille
Ⓣ 01 72 29 35 35
operadeparis.fr
⊕ 12/V13

Atelier de Paris
Cartoucherie de Paris, 12th
Ⓜ Château de Vincennes
Ⓣ 01 41 74 17 07
atelierdeparis.org
⊕ Off map

Centre National de la Danse
1 r Victor Hugo,
93507 Pantin
Ⓜ Hoche
Ⓣ 01 41 83 27 27
cnd.fr
⊕ Off map

Cours Florent
37-39 av Jean Jaurès, 19th
Ⓜ Jaurès
Ⓣ 01 40 40 04 44
coursflorent.fr
⊕ 4/W2

Ecole Jacques Lecoq
57 r du Fbg St-Denis, 10th
Ⓜ Gare de l'Est
Ⓣ 01 47 70 44 78
ecole-jacqueslecoq.com
⊕ 7/R6

10

Bibliothèque Nationale de France
Site François Mitterand, quai François Mauriac, 13th

Studios and residences

104, Cent Quatre
(opens spring 2008)
104 r d'Aubervilliers, 19th
Ⓜ Riquet
then 104.fr
✛ 4/U1

**Centre International
d'Accueil et d'Echanges
de Récollets**
150 r du Fbg St -Martin, 10th
Ⓜ Gare de l'Est
Ⓣ 01 53 26 21 00
centre-les-recollets.com
✛ 3-4/T4

**Cité Internationale
des Arts**
18 r de l'Hôtel de Ville, 4th
Ⓜ Pont Marie
Ⓣ 01 42 78 71 72
citedesartsparis.net
✛ 11/S12

Cité Internationale Universitaire de Paris
17 bd Jourdan, 14th
Ⓜ Cité Universitaire
Ⓣ 01 44 16 64 00
ciup.fr
⊕ Off map

Direction des Affaires Culturelles de la Ville de Paris
31 r des Francs Bourgeois, 4th
Ⓜ Hôtel de Ville
paris.fr
⊕ 11-12/T11

Kadist Art Foundation
21 r des Trois Frères, 18th
Ⓜ Abbesses
Ⓣ 01 42 51 83 49
kadist.org
⊕ 3/O2

Les Mains d'Oeuvres
1 r Charles Garnier, 93400 St Ouen
Ⓜ Porte de Clignancourt
Ⓣ 01 40 11 25 25
mainsdoeuvres.org
⊕ Off map

Le Pavillon
Palais de Tokyo, 13 av du Président Wilson, 16th
Ⓜ Iéna
Ⓣ 01 47 23 38 86
palaisdetokyo.com
⊕ 7/O9

Point Ephémère
200 quai de Valmy, 10th
Ⓜ Stalingrad
Ⓣ 01 40 34 02 48
pointephemere.org
⊕ 4/U3

Resources and supplies

Bibliothèque Nationale de France
Site François Mitterrand, quai François Mauriac, 13th
Ⓜ Bibliothèque
Ⓣ 01 53 79 59 59
bnf.fr
⊕ 16/V17

BiFi
51 r de Bercy, 12th
Ⓜ Bercy
Ⓣ 01 71 19 32 32
bifi.fr
⊕ 16/X17

BPI/Bibliothèque Kandinsky
Centre Pompidou, 4th
Ⓜ Rambuteau
Ⓣ 01 44 78 12 33
centrepompidou.fr
⊕ 11/Q10

Dubois
20 r Soufflot, 5th
Ⓡ Luxembourg
Ⓣ 01 43 54 43 60
dubois-paris.com
⊕ 15/O15

SACD
5 r Ballu, 9th
Ⓜ Place de Clichy
Ⓣ 01 40 23 45 20
sacd.fr
⊕ 2/L3

Sennelier
3 quai Voltaire, 7th
Ⓜ St Germain des Prés
Ⓣ 01 42 60 72 15
magasinsennelier.com
⊕ 10/M11

10

See page 9 to scan the directory

INDEX

Page numbers in italics refer to chapter directories

11

11

187

11

Péniche Opéra
Quai de Loire, 19th

11

Château Rouge

esses

Barbès-Rochechouart

Le Chapelle

Stalingrad

4

19th

Ourcq

Laumière

igalle

Anvers

Gare Du Nord

Eurostar Thalys

Louis Blanc

daurès

Bolivar

St-Georges

Poissonnière

Château-Landon

Colonel Fabien

Buttes Chaumont

Botzaris

Cadet

Gare De L'est

Jourdain

e-de-te

Le Peletier

10th

Château D'eau

Pyrénées

ichelieu-Drouot

9th

Grands Boulevards

Bonne Nouvelle

Strasbourg Saint-Denis

8

Jacques Bonsergent

Belleville

Couronnes

re

Bourse

Sentier

République

Goncourt

Ménilmontant

2th

Réaumur Sébastopol

Temple

Parmentier

St-Maur

Etienne Marcel

Arts-et-Métiers

Oberkampf

Père Lachaise

1st

Les Halles

Rambuteau

3th

Filles Du Calvaire

St-Sébastien Froissart

St-Ambroise

11th

re

Louvre-Rivoli

12

Richard Lenoir

Philippe-Auguste

Pont-Neuf

Châtelet

Hôtel de Ville

4th

Chemin-Vert

Bréguet Sabin

Voltaire

Cité

St-Paul

Charonne

billon

Saint-Michel

Pont-Marie

Bastille

Boulets-Montreuil

déon

Cluny-la-Sorbonne

Sully Morland

Ledru-Rollin

Faidherbe-Chaligny

Maubert-Mutualité

16

Cardinal Lemoine

Quai De La Rapée

Gare de Lyon

Reuilly-Diderot

5th

Luxembourg

Jussieu

Montgallet

Place Monge

Gare D'austerlitz

12th

ugommier

ort Royal

Censier Daubenton

St-marcel

Bercy

Maps

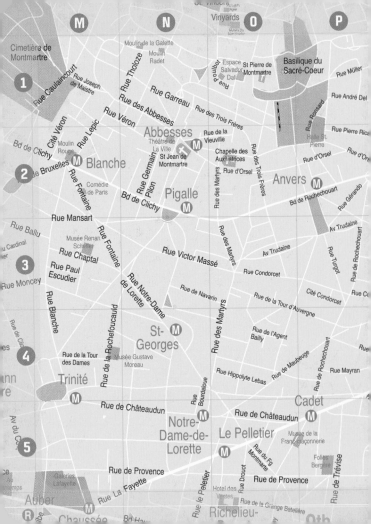

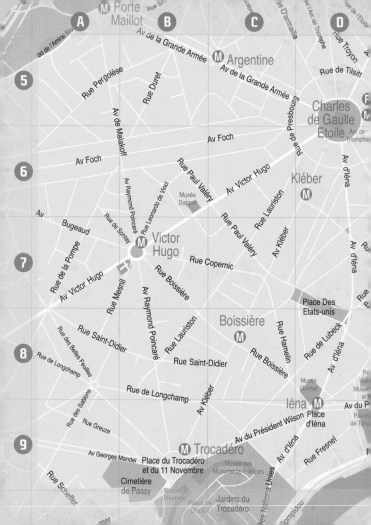

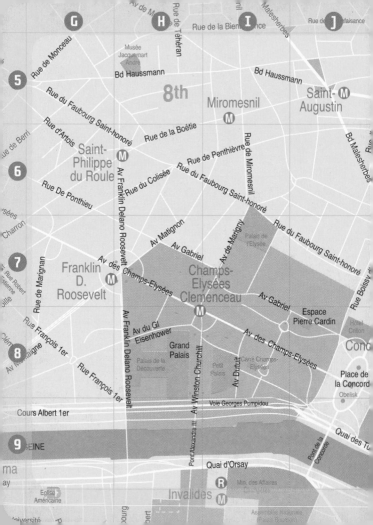

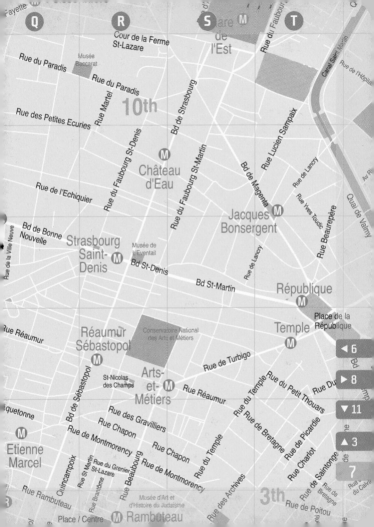

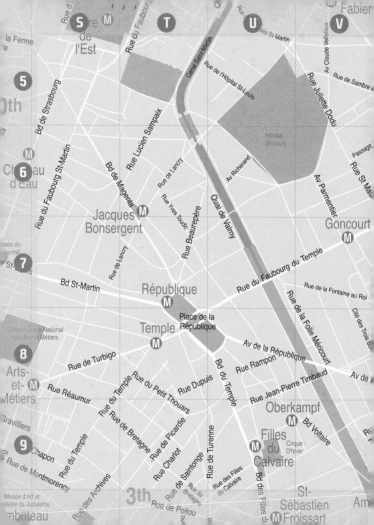

PARIS MET

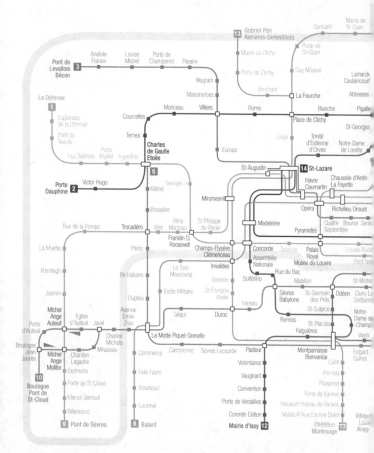

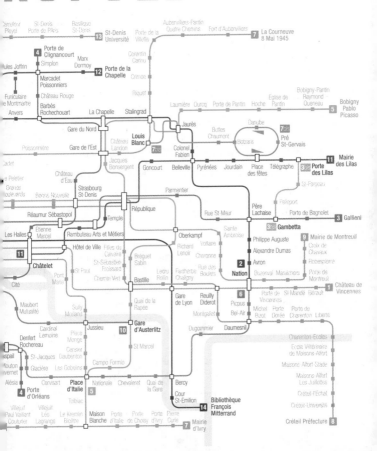

OTHER TITLES IN THE AUTHENTIK COLLECTION

Europe
Gourmet Paris
Chic Paris

Chic London
Gourmet London
Artistik London

FORTHCOMING AUTHENTIK GUIDES – SPRING 2008

North America	Europe	Asia	Africa
Gourmet New York	Barcelona	Beijing	Marrakech
Chic New York	Berlin	Bali	Cape Town
Artistik New York	Milan		
	Prague		

FORTHCOMING WINE ROADBOOKS – AUTUMN 2008

France	Italy	North America
Bordeaux	Tuscany	Napa Valley
Burgundy		Sonoma County
Champagne	Spain	
Loire Valley	Rioja	

Visit www.authentikbooks.com
to find out more about AUTHENTIK titles

K

Natasha Edwards

After working in the art and architecture press in London, Natasha Edwards moved to Paris in 1992. For more than a decade she edited the cultural listings magazine *Time Out Paris*. A specialist in the Paris gallery scene, she contributes regularly to the art and design magazines *Contemporary*, *Blueprint* and *Design Week*. Natasha also writes on French art, culture, food and travel for *The Independent*, *The Daily Telegraph*, *Condé Nast Traveller* and *Elle Decoration*.

Alain Bouldouyre

Gentleman artist Alain Bouldouyre captures in his fine line drawings what our *Artistik Paris* author conjures up in words – the quintessence of the city. Art director for *Senso* magazine, and author/illustrator of numerous travel books, Alain fast tracks around the world in hand-stitched loafers, a paintbox and sketch pad his most precious accessories.

COMMERCIAL LICENSING
Authentik illustrations, text and listings are available for commercial licensing at www.authentikartwork.com

ORIGINAL ARTWORK
All signed and numbered original illustrations by Alain Bouldouyre published in this book are available for sale. Original artwork by Alain Bouldouyre is delivered framed with a certificate of authenticity.

CUSTOM-MADE EDITIONS
Authentik books make perfect, exclusive gifts for personal or corporate purposes.

Special editions, including personalized covers, excerpts from existing titles and corporate imprints, can be custom produced.

All enquiries should be addressed to Wilfried LeCarpentier at wl@authentikbooks.com